Delicate Threads

DELICATE THREADS

Friendships

between Children

with and without

Special Needs

in Inclusive

Settings

Debbie Staub, Ph.D.

Woodbine House 1998

Research for this book was supported in part by the Consortium for Collaborative Research on Social Relationships, Cooperative Agreement #H086A20003, awarded to Syracuse University from the Office of Special Education Programs, U.S. Department of Education. However, the opinions expressed herein are not necessarily those of the U.S. Department of Education, and no official endorsement should be inferred.

Cover Illustration: Amy Tkac

Library of Congress Cataloging-in-Publication Data

Staub, Debbie.
    Delicate threads : Friendships between children with and without special needs in inclusive settings / by Debbie Staub.
    p.   cm.
    Includes bibliographical references and index.
    ISBN 0-933149-90-5 (pbk.)
    1.   Friendship in children. 2. Handicapped children—Attitudes.
I. Title.
HQ784.F7.S74 1998
302.3'4'083—dc21   98-9527
                                      CIP

Manufactured in the United States of America

10 9 8 7 6 5 4 3 2 1

To Ben, Willie, and Carly,

who have taught me about the importance

of friendships in one's life,

and to Tom,

who is my best friend.

Table of Contents

Acknowledgments

The creation of almost anything is seldom a sole endeavor and *Delicate Threads* is no exception. If it hadn't been for the children, parents, teachers, and school administrators who graciously gave of their time, feelings, and stories, I wouldn't have been able to tell the seven tales of friendship presented here. With great gratitude, I thank you all.

I would also like to acknowledge the support and encouragement to write this book that I received from my colleagues and friends from the Consortium for Collaborative Research on Social Relationships of Children and Youth with Diverse Abilities. Luanna Meyer, the director for the Consortium, has paved the way for research on relationships between children with and without special needs. A special thanks is also offered to the co-directors of the Consortium: Marguita Grenot-Scheyer, Beth Harry, Hyun-Sook Park, and Ilene S. Schwartz, and to the Consortium's project officer, Anne Smith. Their intellect and insight provided me with immeasurable resources. More importantly, their friendship reinforced the importance of friends in my own life.

Gratitude is extended also to colleagues who played a significant role in the creation of this book. To Katie Deno, Chrysan Gallucci, Vivien Garza, and Charles Peck, thank you for your belief and faith in me!

Writing a book requires a sense of discipline and commitment. The members of my writing group challenged my ability to stay focused and determined. They also provided opinions, edits, and feedback that were incredibly helpful. They too have unwittingly become part of my friendship circle: Sven Peter Couch, Sara Gage, Rose Mary Mechem Gordon, Sheila Kelly, Nancy Reichley, Jim Teeters, Fritz Wolf, and Rachel Zimmer, and to the memory of Marilyn Osterman, whose life and death have touched me deeply.

I would also like to thank Susan Stokes, my editor, and the folks at Woodbine House for their assistance and vision in seeing this book through.

Finally, I couldn't write a book about friendships without thanking the friends in my life who provide me with laughter, love, respect, and emergency child care! Carolyn, Janet, Eric, Kevin, Jeff, Lisa, Felicia, Jennifer, and especially Tom, thank you!

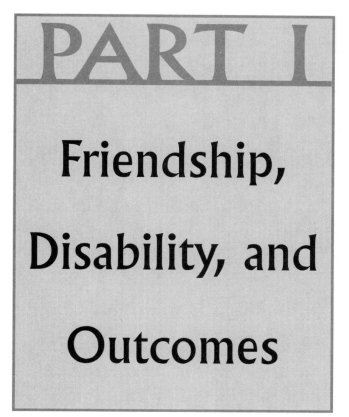

PART I

Friendship, Disability, and Outcomes

Chapter 1

Introduction

"However true love may be, it is less so than friendship."
(Francois de la Rochefoucauld)

Friendship, and having friends, is an essential part of being human. Friends are vitally important in our lives. Many of my fondest and happiest memories are of times spent in the company of friends. My most anguished and despairing times occurred when a friend was sick or dying, when I had no friend to turn to in moments of personal crisis, or when I was a stranger in a strange place and hadn't yet made any friends. Many books, songs, plays, movies, and poems have been written about friendship. Friendship comes in various forms and styles, and it has many different meanings. An individual may have just one "best friend" and that may be enough, or may be surrounded by friends and that may not be enough. Our friendships are precious to us, whether they be few or many.

The value of friendship is no less important in childhood than it is in adulthood. Just as adults rely on their friends for companionship, support, love, and validation, children rely on their friends for the very same reasons. Children develop ideas about what a friend is at very early ages. By the time they reach preschool age, most children have at least one special person in their lives whom they consider a "friend." Children develop friends in their neighborhoods, through family functions, at church and other community settings, and in school. Since school-age children spend a good proportion of their time at school, it isn't surprising that the classroom is a place where children make, keep, and lose friends. Many of our life-long lessons about social relationships with others occur in the classroom and at school.

If you asked a teacher or school administrator whether they thought children's relationships with their peers played an important role in a child's educational experience, most would agree, that to some extent, they do. In fact, much of the current curriculum pedagogy and theory is based on the concept of getting children to work together, interact, resolve conflict, and basically co-exist peacefully. We have become very aware of the problems that occur when we do not acknowledge and respect differences that children bring to the classroom. In efforts to prevent racial discrimination, gang activity, and violent and criminal behavior in children, educators, researchers, and even politicians are struggling to find interventions and programs that teach children how to get along, how to respect each other's differences, and how to work cooperatively. Furthermore, there is an extensive body of research that indicates that participating in meaningful relationships is a critical part of a typical child's development and well-being and that friendships help protect children from adjustment problems later in life.

While we have understood for some time now the value of friendship for typically developing children, only recently have educators and researchers begun to explore the benefits and meaning of friendship for children with cognitive disabilities. Over the past decade in special education, researchers and educators have begun to recognize the importance of friendship for children with disabilities and have gone to great pains to provide opportunities for children with disabilities to develop meaningful friendships with their nondisabled peers. We still have a long way to go in our work regarding friendships between children with and without disabilities, but further study of these friendships seems especially critical in light of the research findings to date.

Christine Hurley-Geffner (1995), who writes about friendships between children with and without developmental disabilities, believes that if researchers are to make advances in their knowledge of friendships between children with and without disabilities, several factors must be considered when designing and conducting such research:

1. *Defining friendship through the use of direct behavioral observation.* That is, spending time objectively observing interactions that children have with one another, repeatedly, over time. Once sufficient observations are made, researchers can begin to identify themes or patterns among the interactions.

2. *Using friendship as the variable of study.* That is, choosing to observe pairs of children who we believe are friends and observing their friendly interactions with one another in particular.

3. *Conducting research on friendship in natural environments.* That is, identifying the places where friends interact—i.e., the classroom, the playground, each other's homes—and observing their interactions in these settings.

4. *Consideration of the relationship and viewing both children as co-creators of their relationship.* That is, having respect for the individual differences that each child brings to the friendship, and, in particular,

identifying what each child receives from and
gives to the friendship.

I have attempted to consider these four factors in my own
work and I believe that the outcomes of my research, shared
here in this book, reflect these considerations.

Background, Participants, and Setting

In January 1993, I was hired to work as a research associate
for the Consortium for Collaborative Research on Social Relationships of Children and Youth with Severe Disabilities. The
Consortium was a five-year federally funded national research
institute designed to study how children and young people from
diverse perspectives and with widely varying abilities and personal characteristics come to form relationships. A particular
interest of the institute was in friendships and social supports
for children and youth with diverse abilities (see Meyer, Park,
Grenot-Scheyer, Schwartz, and Harry, 1998). The Consortium
for Collaborative Research on Social Relationships had several research sites in different regions of the United States
which reflected the diverse demographic realities of schools
and communities in our country. I served as a research coordinator at several sites in the Pacific Northwest, including at
Jane Austen Elementary School, which is located in a suburban neighborhood in the Pacific Northwest.

Guided by the work and research of the Consortium, I
became interested in studying the friendships between children with and without disabilities in elementary classrooms. I
chose to study those friendships in classrooms considered to
be fully included. I consider a classroom to be "fully included"
when the following key elements are evident[1]:

---

[1] Adapted from Sailor, W., Gee, K., & Karasoff, P. (1993). Full inclusion and school
restructuring. In M. Snell (Ed.), *Systematic instruction of persons with severe
handicaps* (4th edition). Columbus: Chas. Merrill.

1. **Full general education class membership for all students.** That is, all students, including students with disabilities, are considered to be a full member of the general education classroom.
2. **Full perception of "ownership" from both special and general education.** That is, both the general and special education teacher assume responsibility for the students with disabilities and work together collaboratively to insure that their needs are being met.
3. **Individual outcomes-based decision making.** That is, decisions regarding the student's educational goals and objectives are based on individual assessment and need.
4. **Student-based services with a team curriculum design.** That is, a team of educators and family work together to develop the student's IEP as well as the curriculum in which the IEP goals and objectives are to be addressed.
5. **Site-team coordination of services and educational support.** That is, all parties who have input regarding the student (i.e., general and special education teacher, parent(s), school psychologist, related services personnel, etc.) work together as a team to provide the necessary support for the accomplishment of the student's IEP goals and objectives.

It is my contention that fully inclusive classrooms offer children with disabilities the greatest opportunity to make friends with their peers. With the inclusion movement has come an explicit effort to identify those settings, situations, and supports that help facilitate meaningful and positive relationships between children with and without disabilities (Harry, etc.). In fact, one of the key elements in defining "full inclusion" is the necessity of support.

Additionally, most of the research in this area has focused on studying the types of supports and strategies that appear effective in fostering friendships between children with and without disabilities. However, the literature shows little evidence of how friendships between children with and without disabilities develop, what they look like and how they are different from or similar to friendships between typically developing children, and what happens to the friendships over time (Meyer, Park, Grenot-Scheyer, Schwartz, and Harry, 1998). These were some of the very questions that I was interested in pursuing. Additional questions I included:

1. In what ways do typically developing children and children with disabilities change as a result of their friendship with each other? What are the mutual benefits they experience from their friendship? What are the potential drawbacks, barriers, or concerns? What happens to children, both those with and without disabilities, who do not have friends?

2. What kinds of meaning do these children bring to their friendships? What meanings do the significant people in their lives attach to these friendships?

3. What kinds of contextual and setting events, such as teacher attitude or classroom design, drive the mutual benefits of these friendships? Can these factors be manipulated or controlled to increase the anticipated benefits for all students?

IDENTIFYING THE "PLAYERS"

In the spring of 1993, I began my research by studying several pairs of children, one with a disability and one without, who were already perceived as friends. I selected the pairs of friends by talking to general education teachers who had children with moderate or severe disabilities attending their fully included classrooms at Jane Austen Elementary School[2]. I asked them to identify typically developing children who seemed to be particularly close (I referred to these children as "connected") to the student with disabilities in their classroom. A total of twenty-one typically developing students and eight different children with disabilities were identified across seven different classrooms. Consequently, the children with disabilities who participated in this study were likely to have more than one typically developing peer identified as "connected" to them. At that time, the children's ages ranged from 6 to 12 years. After the initial identification of the twenty-one "connected pairs" (one child with a disability and one without), I began preliminary observations of the children's interactions. I also interviewed the typically developing children, their parents, their teachers, and the parents of the children with disabilities. My purpose for these early activities was to get to know the children on a deeper level and determine whether the relationships that existed between the pairs of children had some substance and were likely to continue. I also wanted to identify pairs of children who were engaging in friendly and companionable interactions the majority of the time. Four of these original pairs of children became the basis for a journal article, "Four portraits of friendship at an inclusive school" (Staub, Schwartz, Gallucci, and Peck, 1994).

By fall of the next school year, I had narrowed the number of pairs of "connected" peers down to seven. I continued to follow three of the pairs of children highlighted in the journal publication. A number of factors were involved in whether or not I continued to follow a pair of children. First, several of the typically developing children had moved away and were no longer attending Jane Austen Elementary. Second, one of the students with disabilities had moved to a new elementary school and one had moved on to junior high school. In a couple of situations, I chose not to follow the "connected peers" because they were no

---

[2] Jane Austen Elementary is a pseudonym. In order to protect the confidentiality of the children involved in this study, pseudonyms have been used for all names.

longer in the same class as their peer with disabilities and it did not appear that they were continuing their relationship outside of the classroom setting. Finally, based on feedback from the interviews and my own observations, I did not feel that some of the pairs of children were engaged in a true friendship. More often than not, the relationship was based on the nondisabled child "helping" the child with disabilities.

A "FRIENDLY" PLACE TO BE

Jane Austen Elementary School is located in a suburban neighborhood in the Pacific Northwest. Approximately 850 children are enrolled in this school, which serves a predominantly Caucasian population. Jane Austen Elementary first became an "inclusive" school in the early 1990s when it set a mission of including students with moderate and severe disabilities as full members into general education classrooms.

Jane Austen Elementary prides itself on being a "community of learners." The philosophy or mission statement developed by its staff, faculty, and community is built on including, supporting, and collaborating to meet the needs of *all* of its students. There are no pull-out or self-contained programs at Jane Austen for students with mild, moderate, or severe disabilities. Rather, all children are served within the general education classroom. The faculty is very committed to providing a curriculum in their classrooms that accommodates all learners. Adaptations to the curriculum are just as likely to occur for "slower" learners as they are to occur for "accelerated" learners. The faculty also uses curriculum technology that reflects best practices in the field of education, such as cooperative learning strategies, multi-age grouping, thematic instruction, and student-directed learning techniques. A sense of equality and cooperation is very evident at Jane Austen. The staff and faculty work hard to make sure that each student feels like a contributing, participating member.

I first became acquainted with the Jane Austen community as a research coordinator for the Consortium of Collaborative Research on Social Relationships. Jane Austen Elementary not only served as one of the Consortium's research sites, but was also where our research office was located. Since I was spending a great deal of time on the Jane Austen campus, I felt particularly fortunate to have many opportunities to get to know not only the pairs of "connected peers" well, but also the classrooms where their friendly interactions were taking place.

Data Collection

To collect the data for this study I used a combination of observations, videotaping, and interviews. Prior to collecting any data, parent consent for participation was obtained for both children with and without disabilities. I also received permission from the classroom teachers and the principal at Jane Austen to spend time "hanging" out in classrooms. Classroom observations were conducted regularly by either myself or a data collector hired to work on the research project. We collected data throughout the entire school year, September to June, over three years for all but two pairs of the connected peers. For two pairs of connected peers, I was only able to collect two years of data because both pairs of children moved on to different junior high schools during the third year of my research.

As observers, my data collectors or myself generally played passive roles in the classroom during the data collection period. However, if a teacher or student asked us for help we would respond willingly. Data from the classroom observations were collected using ethnographic field notes. That is, data collectors were trained to collect both written, objective descriptions of the children's behaviors and interactions, as well as analytic notes, which were interpretations and judgments about what we felt about the meaning of these behaviors. The observations ranged in length from 15 to 45 minutes, and usually one or two observations were conducted every week. Three types of observations were completed: 1) observations with the child with disabilities as the focus, 2) observations of the child without disabilities as the target, and 3) general classroom observations. In many instances, there was overlap. For example, if I was observing the child with disabilities as the target and she was playing with their identified connected peer, I would certainly base my observations and opinions on their interactions together.

Videotaped samples of the school day were also used to gather information for this study. These samples were collected at the beginning and the end of the school year. The video samples were collected with the child with disabilities as the focal point across the child's school day to represent a balance of activities. The video samples were used as an additional source of observational data. If I found video footage that included interactions between the pair of "connected peers," I would analyze the video and write observations and anecdotal information regarding their interactions.

The third type of data that I collected to build "case studies" of the pairs of connected peers were semi-structured interviews. Interviews with the children without disabilities were conducted either by myself or one of my data collectors with whom the children were well acquainted and very comfortable. I also conducted interviews with the parents of the children with and without disabilities, their classroom teachers, and special education instructional assistants.

The interview questions were different for each group of respondents but there were some similarities. For example, I used open-ended questions for all of the interviews and I always began each interview with a grand tour question (e.g., "Tell me about your friendship with Molly.") Additional questions were asked to gain more information about the friendship between the children with and without disabilities in my attempt to unpack the meaning of the relationship as perceived by the interviewee. In preparing the questions for the interview, specific questions for individual children were developed based on vignettes pulled from the classroom observations. For example, if the classroom observation notes had described an incident where Aaron (a child without disabilities) had negotiated a different set of rules for his friend Cole (a child with severe cognitive delays) to play in a recess game, I might ask Aaron specific questions related to this incident such as, "Why did you do this" or "How did your classmates react to your suggestion to change the rules for Cole?"

In all of the interviews, respondents were asked to provide examples to elaborate their responses, and follow-up questions were asked when appropriate to gather more information. The interviews with the adults ranged in length from 45 to 90 minutes. The interviews with the children ranged in length from 10 to 30 minutes. All interviews were audiotaped and then later transcribed. Initial interviews were conducted with all of the 21 children without disabilities who had been nominated as "connected peers" in the spring. We continued to interview the remaining seven children without disabilities each spring for the next couple of years to note differences in their friendship with the child with disabilities. Yearly interviews were also conducted with parents, teachers, and the instructional assistants.

While some of the children we interviewed were a bit shy and hesitant, for the most part, all of the adults I interviewed were very forthcoming and outspoken during their interviews. By the end of the three years I felt very comfortable with them and I think they did with me as well. I feel very grateful to the parents, staff, and children who so generously gave their time and eloquently expressed their feelings, ideas, and experiences about these important and unique friendships. I was often struck by how enthusiastic and positive these individuals felt about these friendships and the impact they had not only on the children's lives, but their own as well.

From the data I collected through the observations, video samples, and interviews over a period of time emerged seven stories of friendship between children with and without disabilities. I use the seven stories of friendship to illustrate not only valuable points about childhood friendship in general, but to guide understanding of the unique value and meaning of friendship between a child who is moderately or severely disabled with a child who is not disabled[3]. This book is organized in a way to introduce the reader to each of the pairs of children, to share knowledge about children's friendships in general, and to specifically share what I have learned about the friendships between children with and without disabilities. With that brief introduction, following are stories about seven pairs of children, each pair woven together by the delicate threads that bind them together in the name of friendship.

References

Hurley-Geffner, C.L. (1995). Friendships between children with and without developmental disabilities. In R.L. Koegel & L.K. Koegel (Eds.), *Teaching children with autism*. Baltimore, MD: Paul H. Brookes.

Meyer, L.H., Park, H.S., Grenot-Scheyer, M., Schwartz, I.S., & Harry, B. (Eds.). (1998). *Making friends: The influences of culture and development*. Baltimore, MD: Paul H. Brookes.

Peck, C.A., White, O., Billingsley, F., & Schwartz, I. (1992). *The inclusive education research project: Toward an empirical understanding of process and outcomes associated with the education of children with moderate and severe disabilities in regular classrooms*. OSEP Grant Proposal.

Staub, D., Schwartz, I.S., Gallucci, C., & Peck, C.A. (1994). Four portraits of friendship at an inclusive school. *Journal of the Association for Persons with Severe Handicaps, 19 (4)*, 314-25.

---

[3] Children referred to in this book as having moderate and/or severe disabilities generally experience mental retardation in the moderate or severe range.

Chapter 2

Delicate Threads:
Seven Stories of Friendship

"Each friend represents a world in us, a world not possibly born until they arrive, and it is only by this meeting that a new world is born." (Anais Nin)

Graduation day for the sixth graders at Jane Austen elementary school promises to be warm and sunny, Fitting weather for a joyful celebration, especially for Molly, a sixth-grade student with Down syndrome who has been anticipating this event for several weeks. The early morning fog has burned away and by 11:00 a.m. it is already 75 degrees—unusual for the Northwest, even in late June. The lunchroom has been converted into an auditorium and chairs have been set out in rows. Laden with video cameras, parents and their young children fill the chairs. Molly's mother, a widow of two years, enters. She is trailed by her four other daughters, all redheads like Molly. Shortly after, Stacy's mother and father enter the room. Stacy's mother looks elegant and cool in spite of the growing heat and her father walks with the confidence of a successful business man. The parents chat amongst themselves while the sixth graders wait impatiently in the hallway to begin the processional march.

Someone dims the lights and music plays as the sixth grade graduates enter the auditorium. They fill the first ten rows of chairs with giggles and whispers. The principal stands at the podium on the makeshift stage and gives his welcome speech, which goes on far too long for these excited sixth graders. Their thoughts are on summer vacation, the graduation cake, and upcoming sixth-grade parties.

As is customary, each of the sixth-grade teachers gives a short speech about their wonderful year and their wonderful kids. Then they call each of their students by name to approach the podium to receive their certificate of elementary school completion. Moms and Dads hurry to the front of the room when they hear their child's name in hopes of a good photo opportunity. Each name called results in a polite spattering of applause and occasional catcalls from classmates.

Mr. Page, Stacy's and Molly's teacher, is the last to hand out diplomas. He tentatively climbs the stairs to the podium and turns a deep shade of red when his students give him a loud and rambunctious welcome. The parents, who have heard of Mr. Page's great popularity, watch him with interest. His long blond hair is neatly tied into a pony tail and his scraggly goatee has been shaved away for the occasion. In spite of his obvious embarrassment, this young teacher of three years breaks into a wide grin as he calls the students up to receive their certificates.

The second name Mr. Page calls is Stacy's. As her classmates cheer her on, Stacy approaches the podium with an elegant grace—she is her mother's daughter. She is dressed in a trendy white-and-blue-striped pant suit, topped with a straw hat covered with flowers, her blue eyes sparkling and her face beaming with a great smile. It is easy to see why she is so well liked by her peers, particularly because of her seeming oblivion to the vision she creates. She is humble and a little bit shy when she accepts her diploma and shakes hands with Mr. Page. Her classmates clap loudly for Stacy and her face turns pink with pleasure.

Back in her chair, Molly smiles with pride at her friend and listens attentively for her own name to be called. When Mr. Page does call her name, Stacy gives her a quick squeeze on the arm and nudges her out of the chair. Molly, wearing blue tights, a plaid jumper dress and brown loafers, with her carrot-top hair combed neatly and closely to her head, walks toward the stage. Molly has come far from her first experience in an inclusive classroom in second grade and she has touched the hearts of many along the way. The audience is quiet as they wait for her ascent. She stumbles only once and there is a brief and silent cry of relief as she makes it to Mr. Page successfully. Tears well in many people's eyes as they watch Molly reject Mr. Page's handshake for a big hug instead. The applause is thunderous. Molly faces the audience as she takes it all in, seeming to recognize the significance of this moment. Mr. Page turns quickly away to brush a tear from his cheek. Molly's mother cries openly, while Stacy's mother dabs away her tears with a white handkerchief. When Molly returns to her chair, she and Stacy hug. This gesture between the two friends shows the respect and love they share for one another.

Celebrating special occasions such as graduations, weddings, and birthdays with our friends is a tradition for many people. Oftentimes it is our friends who know best our intimate thoughts and feelings, our struggles and joys as we make our way through life and reach the milestones that accompany our journey. Completing elementary school and moving on to junior high school is one of those milestones for many children. For Molly, a 12-year-old girl with moderate mental retardation, graduating from elementary school with her typically developing classmates was one of the most important events in her young life. The fact that this event and celebration were shared with her dearest friend, Stacy, illustrates the value and importance of friendship for *all* children.

The Importance of Friendships

Friendships are among the most significant parts of children's lives, from age three (and sometimes even earlier) through adolescence. Friendships occupy, both in their actual activities and in the world of thought and fantasy, a large proportion of a child's waking hours. They are often the source of a child's greatest pleasures and deepest frustrations. For many children, going to school each morning is not so much about learning as it is an opportunity to see friends. The difference between a child with even one close friend and a child who wants to make friends but has none can be the difference between a child who is happy and a child who is distressed in one large area of their life (Rubin, 1980).

Friendships with peers are often the key to a child's sense of self-identity and emotional security. Being in the presence of a close friend is often comforting and pleasurable. Being in the company of a group of friends can help children gain a sense of community and belonging. Most importantly, friends provide companionship. A friend is someone who can share both the good times and the difficult moments. A friend is someone a child can trust. Friendly experiences with peers who are similar in age help children to develop an awareness about themselves and provide a better understanding of social reality than family experience alone can give.

Friendships not only provide companionship, but can also create a context for the development of many different social behaviors. Friendships have been found to promote social development, including complex forms of play (Gottman & Parkhurst, 1980), social communication, group entry, cooperation, and impulse control (Hartup & Sancilio, 1986). Researchers have also found that children who are familiar with each other initiate more interactions with their peers, have more social interactions, and interact in ways that are cognitively more mature (Hurley-Geffner, 1995).

Intimate friendships give rise not only to self-acceptance, trust, and rapport, but also to insecurity, jealousy, and resentment. Experiences with this range of emotions may have a large impact on children's later relationships, including their orientations toward friendship and love as adults. As children, friends often teach us things that adults do not or cannot within the context of the adult-child relationship. Children learn how to dominate, protect, assume responsibility, reciprocate, appreciate another's point of view, and arrive at solid conclusions about their own competencies and attributes through their interactions with their peers. Friends can also provide instruction in important areas of life such as managing aggression or sexual relationships (Fine, 1981). Additionally, meaningful relationships and friendships with peers have been found to help children mediate stress in their lives (Cobb, 1976).

Friendship seems to influence reasoning ability. In one study, child development researchers found that when children were placed in conflict situations with either friends or nonfriends, the level of interaction and discussion was greater between the children who were friends than the children who were not friends (Nelson & Aboud, 1985). They also found that the discussion and interaction between the friends was more likely to lead to positive changes in future interactions as well as more mature attitudes toward solving the conflict.

There are many developmental, psychological, and sociological reasons for supporting childhood friendships between typically developing children. These same important reasons can be given for supporting friendships between children with and without significant disabilities. In fact, research has found that for children with disabilities: 1) friendships promote their social development (Asher & Gottman, 1981) and provide the opportunity to develop, practice, and maintain a variety of communicative, cognitive, and social-emotional skills; 2) peer relationships provide the context to practice and master the social rules that govern how we use these skills and behaviors across a variety of settings (Meyer, 1996); 3) friendships serve important emotional functions by providing children with nurturance, support, and security (Asher & Gottman, 1981); and 4) friendships may form a network of relationships that allow children with significant disabilities to grow up, go to school, and live, work, and recreate within communities of their choice (Grenot-Scheyer, 1990).

Seven Stories of Friendship

The importance of friendship is reflected in each of the seven stories shared in this book. Each story illustrates the nature of friendship between children in general and the unique value and meaning of friendships between children with and without significant disabilities. A better understanding of the significance of these relationships from the perspectives of the children themselves will perhaps enhance our own abilities as teachers, parents, and other concerned adults to create and facilitate environments and practices that support these valuable relationships.

MOLLY AND STACY

When Stacy got off the bus from kindergarten six years ago, her mother found her in tears.

"Why are you so sad?" her mother asked.

"That girl, the one without any hair, hugged me today. Darrin told me that I'm going to be bald just like her because she touched me."

Stacy's mother patiently explained to her distraught daughter that you couldn't "catch" baldness. She emphasized that Molly's baldness was due to a problem that only Molly had, a type of rare vitamin deficiency.

A year later, Stacy and her mother had a similar conversation after Stacy once again got off the school bus crying. This time Molly had kissed Stacy and Stacy was convinced that she was going to catch whatever it was that Molly had. What Molly had, Stacy's mother explained, was Down syndrome. It was something that Molly was born with and you couldn't catch it like you could a cold or the chicken pox. Stacy, still wary and uncertain about her feelings toward Molly, completed her first-grade school year without any more run-ins with her.

During the summer before her second-grade year, Stacy was tested and accepted into a gifted program that was separate from the regular school curriculum at Jane Austen Elementary. Linda, Stacy's mother, shared her feelings about Stacy's acceptance into the special program: "My husband and I weren't sure that we wanted her to go full time [to the gifted program] and we did a lot of talking to the teachers, the principal, and other parents and we eventually decided that we didn't want her to participate because we did not want her in an isolated classroom away from her friends where she would feel different from everybody else."

After a lot of discussion, Stacy's parents made what they called a monumental decision: "My husband and I decided not to send Stacy to a gifted program, but to keep her in her regular second-grade class. And guess who her seat partner was? It was Molly! We were blown away because here was this kid of ours that we decided not to send to a gifted program, but her seat partner couldn't read or write. We were a little chagrined by the whole thing." Stacy's parents met with the principal to share their concerns. The principal at Jane Austen explained about the new inclusion program beginning that year and gently reminded them that discussion of inclusion at Jane Austen and "preparation" for it had been going on for at least a year. Linda realized, "While they [the staff and teachers at Jane Austen] were getting inclusion up and going at Jane Austen, we had had every opportunity to express our opinions and we didn't. So we decided we'd better go with the program."

It was in their second-grade year together that Molly and Stacy became friends. Linda describes it as a significant moment in Stacy's life: "For Stacy it was a turning point. I mean I don't know if a seven-year-old can have a turning point in their life, but I think it was for her. Their friendship was a connection immediately and it wasn't something that we could explain to Stacy in kindergarten or in first grade. We couldn't explain to Stacy about Molly, but she found out for herself. In spite of us, the kids wanted this relationship to happen and it did."

When they stand side by side, Molly and Stacy provide quite a contrast to one another. Stacy is a beautiful 12-year-old girl who handles herself with charm and grace unusual for her age. Her blond hair, big blue eyes, and delicate nose suggest a Scandinavian heritage, as does her thin, tall athletic build. Only when her hair is pulled back does one notice the small flaw—her left ear sticking out in an awkward position. But it isn't her appearance that draws attention. Rather, it is her soft voice, her calm manner, her slight blush at a compliment directed her way. She is the perfect student without the boastfulness. She is the modest friend without the self-serving ego. She quietly leads her peers without dictating. She is as intrinsically good as the "Wizard of Oz's" Glinda the "good witch" but without the patronizing voice and magic wand. She is a friend to many but especially to Molly—Molly who blasts into a room with her carrot-top hair and her disheveled clothes looking for mischief. Like Glinda, Stacy places Molly on the path of "goodness" with a calm, knowing maturity. She whispers softly in Molly's ear, reminding her to behave and act like a sixth grader should. Stacy watches with pride as Molly responds to her quiet, respectful reminders.

Unlike Stacy, Molly is short for her 12 years and her hunched-over posture makes her look even smaller than she actually is. She is a mischievous munchkin to Stacy's Glinda. No longer bald, she has straight red hair that hangs almost to her shoulders. Molly dresses conservatively—a bit on the old-fashioned side. Molly's older sister and two younger ones attend a private Catholic school that requires them to wear uniforms and Molly often has that same private school uniform look. She is often shy and it is difficult to understand her mumbled, quiet speech. However, she has effectively learned how to use this shy, coy behavior to her advantage, particularly with the adults around her. It takes you by surprise then when she suddenly grabs at your earrings or glasses so that she can have a better look at them. Before you have time to reprimand her, she gives you a hug and looks at you with her big brown eyes brimming with innocence. But Stacy and many of her classmates have learned all about Molly's tricks and they expect her to behave like a sixth grader, even though she is not at the same academic level as they are. Molly's reading level is close to that of a first-grade student, although she has learned by sight all of her sixth-grade classmate's names. Her math skills are at a practical level; she is able to perform basic computations for shopping and other functional activities. She is able to use a calculator to perform some easy computations and is learning some rudimentary money and time skills. She regularly sees a communication specialist who works with her on her articulation and speech volume. Molly's fine motor skills have really improved over the years and her handwriting is fairly legible. Her gross motor abilities, while occasionally awkward and clumsy, are also improving with time.

Molly and Stacy have the longest-standing friendship among the seven pairs of friends that I followed. Even though they have moved on to different junior high schools, they remain close. They call each other on the phone regularly and visit as often as they can. Their families have developed a relationship with each other as well. Stacy, her mother, father, and younger sister all attended Molly's mother's recent wedding. Molly's father had died suddenly when she was in fourth grade. Stacy and her family were a great source of support to Molly and her mother during this difficult time.

Molly's and Stacy's story highlights the importance of having friendship. From second through sixth grades, each provided the other with companionship, comfort, fun, emotional security, and love. Given the support and commitment from both Molly's and Stacy's families, their friendship is likely to continue for some time.

KARLY AND DEANNE

Karly and Deanne, like Stacy and Molly, also had a friendship that lasted several years. Karly, now 10 years of age and Deanne, 9, first became friends when Karly was a first grader and Deanne was a kindergartener. At the time, they were both attending Caresville, a multi-age classroom for children in kindergarten through second grade within Jane Austin Elementary.

Karly is a shy, hesitant child with Down syndrome who moves slowly and cautiously. Unlike Karly, who doesn't budge unless she has to, Deanne is a flurry of movement. As she bounces from one activity to the next she seems impatient; or maybe, as her teacher suggests, she has a limited attention span.

Given their contrasting appearances and behaviors, it was not obvious why Karly and Deanne were drawn to each other. But closer examination revealed two girls who were timid, hesitant, and often overwhelmed by the activity that surrounded them. Karly's and Deanne's friendship lasted for approximately two years. When Karly entered third grade she and Deanne were no longer in the same class and they eventually lost contact. We will learn more about Karly, Deanne, and their relationship in the next chapter, as their story is used to illustrate the five stages in the life of a friendship.

KARLY AND HENRY

When Karly attended Caresville, she was also friends with a boy named Henry. It was not until they moved to the same third-grade class together, however, that their friendship really blossomed. By that time they had both matured socially and cognitively. They had effectively learned the "skills" of friendship maintenance. They had also become best friends. Their story will be used in Chapter 4 to describe the importance of having a best friend and the skills necessary to maintain this important type of relationship.

Henry is the same age as Karly and experiences mild learning disabilities. Like Karly, he receives special education services within the general education classroom for approximately 45 minutes a week. Karly and Henry also attend a weekly speech therapy session together with a communication specialist. Henry is a dark-haired boy whose looks reflect his mother's Irish-American heritage and his father's Filipino one. Henry is always dressed neatly with a quiet blue or green polo shirt tucked nicely into his khaki pants. His hair is cut short and combed to the right side. His belt matches his faux leather shoes. Although he has that "preppy" rich kid look, his parents struggle to make ends meet. This is a second marriage for both of them and Henry has two half brothers well into their twenties. In essence Henry is an only child. Henry's mother works full time as a postal worker and his father has been out of work due to a back injury for a couple of years. Although it is not easy to understand Henry's father's halting English, it is clear how much his father and mother love Henry and want him to be successful. Their determination to see Henry do well may in part explain Henry's worried behavior and solemn expression. He becomes easily upset at school when things are not going smoothly. During these stressful times Henry finds solace in his friendship with Karly.

AARON AND COLE

Aaron is a typically developing 12-year-old who might be described as a "boy's boy." Not yet interested in girls or other sixth-grade trivia such as who likes whom, Aaron can be found in his classroom surrounded by other male classmates joking and goofing around. At home his mother has to "almost hogtie him to keep him in the house long enough to get his chores done," as he would much rather be off riding his bicycle or building tree forts. Aaron is one of the physically larger students in his class and dresses in a standard daily uniform of jeans and T-shirts. His hair is cut short in the current style, but most of the time it is covered up with a baseball cap, which his teacher is constantly reminding him to take off when he's inside the school building.

Aaron attends a fifth- and sixth-grade multi-age classroom with Cole, a 13-year-old student with severe disabilities. Like Aaron, Cole is a child who enjoys goofing around and laughing with his peers. Although Cole appears to be physically different from the other boys in the class due to his small build and awkward gait, he is definitely a member of his class. Cole's mother, who wants him to be accepted by his peers to the greatest extent possible, dresses him carefully in the right clothes with all the right names. With his "Nike" sneakers, "Big Dog" T-shirts and "501" jeans, he looks like the typical sixth grader. Cole's love of laughter is very endearing to both his peers and the adults who work with him. It is hard to stay angry at Cole in spite of his frequent outbursts and noncompliance to instructions and routines at home and in the classroom.

At 11 months of age, Cole contracted spinal meningitis. Once a typically developing infant, Cole now experiences severe mental retardation and a serious seizure disorder. His "good" and "bad" days are often determined by his rate of seizure activity and the effects of the medication he must take to control them. While Cole has strong social initiation skills, he has a limited expressive vocabulary and does not do any traditional academic work.

Without prompting from adults, Aaron helps Cole with his work, and he watches out for him. Cole and Aaron also hang out together. Mr. Howard, their teacher, discusses what having each other for a friend means to the boys: "With Aaron, he gets this guy that he can walk up to and who says 'Aaron!' and they sit and they have lunch together and Aaron can be with his friends and say 'I'm going to play football now, Cole' and Cole can watch and play out in the field and get run over—which he loves!" Although Cole and Aaron moved on to different junior high schools after their sixth-grade year, Aaron's mother believes that the boys' relationship will have a life-long effect on Aaron. Aaron's and Cole's story, discussed further in Chapter 5, is only one of the many in this book that illustrates the mutual benefits that children experience from friendship.

RAY AND BRITTANY

Ray's and Brittany's story also reveals a mutually reciprocal relationship, although the benefits for them were quite different than those found for Aaron and Cole. Even though she is quite petite, when Brittany enters the classroom, you know she is present. Her personality, charged with optimism and joy, can lighten the atmosphere of any room. Often described by the adults who know her as "cute as a button," Brittany has shoulder-length red hair, twinkling green eyes, and a huge smile that really does seem to reach "ear to ear." She looks smaller than she actually is due to her oversized clothes that look like they were hurriedly pulled together without much attention to style or detail. This is fitting for her nonconformist attitude. Brittany is described by her teacher as a "free spirit who doesn't have a lot of friends and doesn't really care. Her feeling is if you can't accept me for who I am, so what! I'll just hang out with whomever likes me for me." Brittany is a typically developing fifth grader who has difficulty with reading, does well in math, and loves any type of science activity—especially those that allow her to explore outside and experience the natural wonder of a beetle bug crawling up her arm or a small toad cupped in her hands. Brittany is also awed by her friend Ray.

Ray is an 11-year-old boy who experiences severe developmental delays caused by a rare genetic disorder, tuberous sclerosis. Ray exhibits many of the typical characteristics associated with tuberous sclerosis, including a rosy, pimply complexion, frequent seizure activity, and self-stimulatory and autistic-like behaviors. Ray is nonverbal and walks with an awkward gait. His communication is very limited and usually only through his screams is he able to communicate a protest or a desire. Including Ray in the general education program has been challenging for his teachers and there is often discussion of how "appropriate" it is to do so. If you asked Brittany, she would tell you otherwise; "If Ray wasn't in Mr. T's class, where else would he go?"

Brittany is concerned about Ray's comfort, emotional well-being, and his rights as an individual person to have equal access to education and to his nondisabled peers. Brittany truly fits the portrait of an altruistic person as far as Ray is concerned. Their story is used to shed light on the issues of altruism and advocacy among children who attend inclusive environments.

CORRIE AND LINDSEY

Lindsey is not usually described as a typical 10-year-old girl. For one thing, she doesn't have a group of same-sex friends with whom she "hangs." For another, she doesn't have any of that lingering "little girl" personality—also common of girls her age. She is already hardened, independent, and occasionally belligerent in the presence of authority figures. Her blonde hair hangs down her back to her waist. She carries twenty or more extra pounds on her tall frame and her body already shows signs of puberty. Her clothes are usually dirty and disheveled. By the time Lindsey entered fourth grade at Jane Austen Elementary, she had attended three other elementary schools. As her charts get moved from school to school, a teacher or counselor learns that Lindsey has mild learning disabilities; her greatest strengths are math and art and her weakest area is reading. They also learn that she lives with a younger sister, an older step-sister, and her mother. There is no mention of a stepfather. At the end of her fifth-grade year at Austen Elementary, Lindsey's family was on the move again. A data collector asked Lindsey about her feelings on the upcoming change. Lindsey's responses revealed her insecurity and low self-esteem:

> **Interviewer:** "I guess it's sort of exciting to go to a new school next year because you will have a chance to meet new friends."
> **Lindsey:** "Yeah, well I'm usually a pain in the butt when it comes to new schools because I hate them."

Interviewer: "Why do you hate new schools?"
Lindsey: "Because I don't have any friends and the first time I came here [Austen] I was a little pain in the rear end. I'd sass back to the teachers and stuff."

While Lindsey recognized that a lack of friends was a big issue in her life, it was difficult to determine whether Corrie minded not having friends in hers. Even though she was 11 when she met Lindsey in their fourth-grade class, Corrie had never had a same-age friend before—someone whom she consistently sought and hung out with. Like Lindsey, Corrie has a personality and appearance that is quite different from the majority of her peers, most of whom seem so intent on fitting in. Her home-permed hair style, outdated clothes, oversized eyeglasses, pudgy figure, and poor articulation tend to accentuate the bizarre behaviors that she occasionally exhibits. Corrie, who has moderate mental retardation, is significantly below grade level in all academic areas but shines during drawing and other art projects. She has attended inclusive classrooms at Jane Austen Elementary School since second grade and has a history of leaving the school grounds and hiding. For this reason, she often has an adult in her company.

Corrie and Lindsey became acquainted in their third-fourth, multi-grade class. Lindsey remembers meeting Corrie on the first day of school and becoming friends with her right then and there. They spent the entire school year eating lunch together and playing at recess. It was a first true friendship for both. Even though they did not attend the same fifth-grade class together, the two girls remained close. Unfortunately, their relationship ended when Lindsey moved more than 30 miles away from Corrie. Although Corrie was more outgoing and vocal with her peers in her sixth grade class than ever before, she did not have a friendship like the one she had with Lindsey. As Corrie's and Lindsey's story reveals, loneliness is a pervasive problem not only for many children with disabilities, but for nondisabled children as well.

THERESA AND NELLE

If you saw them standing next to each other, you could easily mistake Nelle and Theresa for sisters. Although Nelle is taller than Theresa, they both share dark, straight hair that falls to their shoulders. Theresa tends to keep her hair plain while Nelle's mom likes her to wear barrettes and bows that coordinate with her outfits. They both dress conservatively, without flash, and the style of their clothes seems younger than the sixth graders they both are. Nelle and Theresa are similar in other ways. They each have only one sister, although Theresa is the older sibling and Nelle is the younger. Their parents, who have become friends with each other through their daughters' relationship, have similar family values and tend to lean on the conservative side with regard to raising their children. Both of the girls are also shy, lack confidence, and rarely assert themselves. In spite of their timid manner, they are both well-liked by their peers. A teaching assistant who works with Nelle, a student with moderate mental retardation, and Theresa, a typically developing child, in their fifth and sixth grade classroom, describes Theresa's interactions with her classmates: "She is not a leader in her group, but she does seem to be well-liked. It seems like she's along on the outside of the group looking in, trying to win their approval, but she is becoming more a part of the group all the time."

While the similarities between Theresa and Nelle are apparent to people who know them well, their differences are even more obvious. Theresa is a voracious reader with her head always in a book, while Nelle does not read and speaks in two- to three-word sentences. Her articulation is poor and unless you know her well, it is difficult to understand her. Theresa is advanced for her age in all academic areas, but because of her love for reading, she does particularly well in her literature-based classroom. Nelle can complete simple math problems using a calculator and uses the computers in her classroom independently. Although she cannot read, Nelle loves nothing more than curling up next to Theresa and listening to her quiet voice read the words from one of the many books found in their classroom.

Nelle has been attending inclusive general education classrooms since her third-grade year. Before, she attended a self-contained classroom for children with moderate and severe disabilities, formerly located on the Jane Austen campus. Even though they weren't assigned to the same third-grade classroom, Theresa's and Nelle's friendship began in the third grade when they first made a connection on the school playground. They were eventually placed in the same fourth-grade class and in keeping with the school's tradition of moving from grade to grade in "families," they have been together in the same class for the past three years. Their friendship has gone through several stages. By their sixth-grade year, Theresa and Nelle both were experiencing difficulties in their relationship. Their teacher and other adults in the classroom were relying more and more on Theresa to take care of Nelle's emotional, social, and academic needs. Theresa only wanted to be Nelle's friend. The adults in their lives had unconsciously created roadblocks to the maintenance of their friendship. Eventually their friendship ended. Their story is used to illuminate the important effect that adults have on children's friendships and the balancing act that is often necessary to assume for supporting these relationships.

Conclusion

The stories introduced in this chapter will be used to illustrate many aspects of childhood friendships, including their importance, the developmental sequence and milestones that children often go through, the skills necessary to maintain friends, and the special qualities of a "best" friend. Friendships are also mutually rewarding and there are unique benefits associated with each of the seven pairs of friendships described. Not all of the stories end happily, however. For some of the children presented in this book, loneliness is a pervasive issue. Also troubling is that some of these delicate friendships have ended because the adults were unable to support and enhance their continuation. The role of the adult in setting up caring and effective classroom and community environments is critical to the outcomes of learning, relationships, and membership for *all* children, as will be revealed throughout these stories and in the last chapters of the book.

References

Asher, S.R. & Gottman, J.M. (1981). *The development of children's friendships.* New York, NY: Cambridge University Press.

Cobb, S. (1976). Social support as a moderator of life stress. *Psychosomatic Medicine, 38,* 300-314.

Fine, G.A. (1981). Friends, impression management, and preadolescent behavior. In S.R. Asher and J.M. Gottman (Eds.), *The development of children's friendships* (29-52). New York, NY: Cambridge University Press.

Gottman, J. & Parkhurst, J. (1980). A developmental theory of friendship and acquaintanceship processes. In W.A. Collins (Ed.), *Minnesota symposia on child psychology* (Vol. 13). Hillsdale, N.J.: Lawrence Erlbaum.

Grenot-Scheyer, M. (1990). *Friendships of children with severe handicaps and their nonhandicapped peers.* Unpublished doctoral dissertation, University of California, Los Angeles.

Hartup, W.W. & Sancilio, M.F. (1986). Children's friendships. In E. Schopler & G.B. Mesibov (Eds.), *Social behavior in autism* (61- 80). New York: Plenum.

Hurley-Geffner, C.M. (1995). Friendships between children with and without developmental disabilities. In R.L. Koegel & L.K. Koegel (Eds.), *Teaching children with autism* (105-125). Baltimore, MD: Paul H. Brookes.

Meyer, L.M. (1996). Social relationships. In H.R. Turnbull & A.P. Turnbull (Eds.), *Improving the implementation of the Individuals with Disabilities Education Act: Making schools work for all of America's children* (427-439). Washington, D.C.: National Council on Disability.

Nelson, J. & Aboud, F.E. (1985). The resolution of social conflict between friends. *Child Development, 56,* 1009-1017.

Rubin, Z. (1980). *Children's friendships.* Cambridge, MA: Harvard University Press.

Chapter
3

A Developmental Perspective on the Beginning and Ending of a Young Friendship

"That's what friendship means: sharing the prejudice of experience."
(Charles Bukowski)

The large room, which functions both as a gymnasium and cafeteria, is congested with hungry children filling their lunch trays with food, utensils, and beverages. Karly picks up a carton of milk, a plastic fork and spoon, and a salad piled high and topped with Thousand Island dressing, then hesitantly walks towards the tables lined in rows. With over 300 noisy, bustling students occupying this space, Karly's hesitancy is understandable. She scans the room looking for a familiar face. Deanne sees Karly and waves her over. Karly smiles with a look of relief and settles down next to her friend. The two girls talk, giggle, eat, and eventually leave for the school playground holding hands.

Outside Karly and Deanne head for the "Big Toy," which is a wooden apparatus made up of several sets of stairs and ladders, ramps, slides, and a tire swing. The tire swing is usually the most popular section of this toy, but today Karly and Deanne are lucky—there isn't a line of kids waiting for their turn on the swing. They spend the rest of their lunch recess together pushing each other on the swing, then laughing as they dizzily try to stand. When the bell rings, signaling the end of recess, they join hands again and skip to their classroom. Their cheeks are flushed from their physical activity and their eyes sparkle with pleasure from their playful interaction. A casual observer might note that this relationship doesn't seem different at all from any other relationships amongst the multitude of other first graders playing together at recess time.

The scene above describes a typical interaction between Karly and Deanne, who were friends for two years. The "ordinariness" of this interaction and their relationship, however, were extraordinary. Although parents of typically developing children are likely to take their children's friendships for granted, many parents of children with moderate and severe disabilities do not. A friendship with another child is often one of the most significant events to happen in their child's life. Karly's attendance at an inclusive elementary school provided her with an opportunity to make friends in a very "normal" way. Karly's and Deanne's relationship with each other included a beginning and an ending. I was able to observe and study the start of their relationship from strangers to best friends, through its deterioration, and eventually its ending. Their story enhances understanding of how children's friendships develop and also reinforces the importance of friendship for all children.

Five *Stages* in the Life of a *Friendship*: A Blueprint

George Levinger and Ann Levinger (1986) have described five stages in the "life" of a friendship from acquaintance to termination. The first stage is the meeting phase or getting acquainted stage. Whether or not two people become acquaintances is determined by their proximity to one another and their opportunities to interact. Setting is another determining factor; it can either hinder a friendship from developing by not giving children enough opportunities to become acquainted, or it can nourish a friendship by providing activities and environments that allow for ample interactions and contact. The second stage in the life of a friendship is the build-up phase. This is the point where children decide whether to take their relationship beyond the stage of acquaintance to a higher level of intimacy. The third stage refers to the time when friendship continues with moderate closeness over a period of time. This is usually the most pleasurable and comfortable stage in a friendship when the friends have gotten to know each other well and there is little conflict between them. The fourth and the final stages of friendship are referred to as deterioration and termination. Although not all friendships will go through all of these changes, these stages offer a blueprint for sharing stories of friendship from a developmental perspective.

BECOMING ACQUAINTED: BUILDING THE FOUNDATION

All friendships begin at the acquaintanceship level. Since friendships require an investment of time and emotion, most children's relationships never get beyond the level of acquaintance. To become acquainted with others, children need opportunities to get to know someone on a more personal level. These opportunities arise when proximity places them close to others and it defines the boundaries within which friend-ships are built.

The story of Karly and Deanne illustrates how an inclu-sive setting can help children with and without disabilties more easily advance to the acquaintance phase of a relationship. It was during her first-grade year in an inclusive program at Jane Austen Elementary that Karly became acquainted with Deanne. Deanne would later become Karly's first friend.

At that time Karly, who has Down syndrome, was a shy, quiet child who had experienced many hardships. At age five she required heart surgery to correct a life-threatening condi-tion. During Karly's recovery, her mother, Beth, was diagnosed with non-Hodgkins cancer. While Beth spent many months hospitalized for treatment, Karly's father and a close family friend cared for her. Now in remission, Beth believes these early experiences led to Karly's current difficulty in express-ing her anger: "Even when she is angry, even if she is mad or whatever, she will not let you see." Whether Karly's withdrawn behavior is due to the traumas in her early years or is a part of her personality is difficult to determine. She has trouble mak-ing transitions between activities and often seems uncomfort-able in her surroundings.

When I first met Karly, she was six and had short curly brown hair and eyeglasses that accentuated her wide-eyed look. Beth reports that she gave up trying to select Karly's outfits years ago, so it is not unusual to find her dressed in a polka dot shirt and striped pants. Karly's awkward appearance, coupled with an air of helplessness, give her the look of a deer caught in the headlights. The nurturing, mothering side of adults and children alike are drawn to Karly and her vulnerability to the world around her. After she has come to trust and know you she will give you a peek into her charming, loving, and sur-prisingly sophisticated sense of humor. It is necessary to be patient. As her mother points out, Karly requires sufficient time to process directions: "She's easily frustrated. If she has an idea she wants to do something and then for some reason it doesn't get processed well for her, she decides she can't do it and gives up."

During her preschool years Karly attended a classroom for children with disabilities. The small class had eight to ten children, staffed by a minimum of two adults. In that setting Karly received physical and speech therapy services. Now in fourth grade, she continues to have speech therapy for approximately one hour a week. She is close to her grade level in reading and spelling. She struggles with math concepts but is able to participate in the general education curriculum with modifications to the assigned activities and with limited support from a special education teaching assistant.

Before she enrolled, Deanne was familiar with Caresville, the multi-age, kindergarten-second-grade classroom that Karly attended, because she often accompanied her mother to the class to pick up her older brother. She had noticed Karly, and while they never interacted, they had played in close proximity on several occasions. Deanne recalled these early experiences: "I met her (Karly) a little last year, when I went to my brother's classroom because my Mom helped out there." When the two girls met formally, Deanne was a kindergartner.

Deanne is a beautiful child with long brown hair. She dresses stylishly and colorfully and walks with a grace that comes from having taken many dance lessons. Deanne's early years have been very different from Karly's troubled ones. Deanne has an older brother and two healthy parents. She enjoys many privileges, such as family vacations to exotic islands, private dance lessons, and the devoted attention of a mother and father who obviously cherish her. "How do I describe Deanne? As my light, my life. I will never tire of watching her every movement," says her mother. Like Karly's parents, Deanne's parents waited until their mid-thirties to raise a family.

Deanne is outgoing with children she knows, but withdrawn around strangers. Although she is at grade level academically, school work doesn't seem to interest her much. Her teachers speculate that in the beginning of kindergarten

Deanne's need for social growth took precedence over her need for academic skill building. Early in her kindergarten year Deanne often played alone or sat on the periphery of a group, appearing uncertain about where she fit in. It is perhaps their shared intimidation of Caresville's active, noisy environment that initially brought Karly and Deanne together.

When Karly and Deanne were placed together in Caresville, the first prerequisite for establishing an acquaintanceship—proximity—was met. Another factor that obviously affects the likelihood of a relationship forming is simple opportunity to interact. The more certain one is of encountering another person again, the more worthwhile it may seem to invest the time necessary to establish a relationship. How close children's homes are to one another, how frequently they can play together, and how close their ages are all contribute to a child's friendship choice. These parameters tend to be out of a young child's control. The choice to interact again and to continue to interact more intensively, however, begins to be based on other cues.

Among neighbors and schoolmates, children tend to interact largely with those who are most like themselves. Similarity in choice of activities, in energy level, and in skills all begin to affect a child's choice of a playmate. Young children typically view their friends as "momentary physical playmates" or whomever they happen to be playing with (Rubin, 1980). They usually think of their friends in terms of physical attributes, rather than in terms of psychological qualities such as personal needs, interests, or character traits. At these early ages, most children do not have a clear idea of an enduring relationship that exists apart from specific encounters.

Children ages five to young adolescence are also most likely to be attracted to peers who are similar to themselves. While attending Caresville placed Karly and Deanne in proximity to one another, it was their similar need for companionship and their shared feelings of being overwhelmed by their busy environment that led them to their first interactions. In very early observations of Karly and Deanne I noticed that the girls were often physically very close to one another during large group activities in the classroom, but seldom spoke with one another. At the same time, their teacher shared her impression of these early meetings: "They mostly sit together, sit on the rug together because in language time they're usually not together and during math they are. Mainly what we see is sitting and touching, sometimes hugging."

As children interact with one another, there is a further "filtering" so that those pairs who become friends are especially likely to have similar activity styles, interests, and values. For Karly and Deanne, several similiarities helped draw them together. They are both observers. They like to watch what is going on before jumping into an activity. When they first met, their shared interests included books, playing on the Big Toy at recess, and playing in the dress-up area.

Since opportunity is an obvious influence on the likelihood of a relationship developing, the extent to which the environment offers, encourages, and supports children's interactions with each other may determine whether or not a relationship will develop. The philosophy of the Caresville teachers promoted social interactions between the children. The classroom setting was designed to allow for natural exchanges. Tables replaced desks, centers were found around the room, and cozy corners and open work areas were filled with busy children. Students moved about freely as they gathered materials and chose places to work. They were seated at tables in groups of four or five and often worked cooperatively together on one activity. The teachers encouraged "table talk" or chatting among the group mates. They also required the students to ask their peers for help before asking an adult. On several occasions Karly and Deanne were assigned to the same table. This proximity to one another provided them with their first opportunities to get to know each other. Eventually their interactions carried over to other times and activities.

"Choice" time was an important opportunity for students to get to know each other in Caresville. During the last hour of the school day the teachers set up five to eight activity "centers" that the Caresville students could choose to play in. The centers were highly interactive, with activities such as building blocks, looking at books in the reading loft, and playing board games. One activity center that Karly and Deanne both liked was the "dress-up" area. Initially the two girls selected this area during choice time independent of the other, although later I observed that they would discuss which area they were going to choose for choice time collaboratively. Often it was the dress-up area.

Most friendships are dependent on the idea that each person in the pair brings something distinctive to the relationship. Consequently, each can learn something from the other. The fact that Karly has a disability was not the defining feature of this relationship nor was the fact that Deanne was friendly with Karly because of the disability. Rather, Karly and Deanne each brought a need for companionship to their classroom environment. The comfort that they provided each other was equally important. At times I observed Deanne nurturing or looking out for Karly, but I saw just as many instances of Karly providing solace to Deanne. Once the two became more confident and the classroom became less intimidating, they had many more playful and silly interactions. Thus, their relationship was founded first on proximity and then on a similar need that they each had. This similar need was a cornerstone of their friendship.

Although proximity and shared interests were the cornerstones of Karly's and Deanne's acquaintanceship, these factors would probably not be as important in the early stages of a friendship between older children. From early childhood to adolescence there is a gradual decrease and then a leveling off of the importance of close proximity for selecting friends. Older children begin to choose friends from broader environments. There are also some differences in same-age selection. Very young children are often in the company of adults or older children, although not necessarily by choice, and therefore may not have a wide selection of possible friends to choose from. Likewise, if they are in traditional graded classrooms, elementary-aged children are often with same-age friends, especially in school settings. Adolescents are able to choose friends from a wider span of age groups as they enter into more situations such as work settings or other community places where age is not a criterion for participation (Epstein, 1989).

BUILDING A FRIENDSHIP: MOVING IN

Within two months of their first year together in Caresville, Karly and Deanne moved beyond the stage of "momentary physical playmates." While proximity and similarity helped Karly and Deanne get to know one another, their relationship was strengthened in a variety of ways typical of other friendships in their age group. Typically, the move from acquaintance to the beginning of friendship is deepened by the understanding that one's presence is important to another person. This is an understanding that both Karly and Deanne clearly reached.

It first became apparent that Karly and Deanne were becoming friends when they began deliberately seeking each other out during large group times. A brief excerpt from the observation notes reveals the subtlety of these early interactions:

> The teacher has called the students over for story. They all move to the big rug area and sit down. Karly sits down next to Deanne. Deanne smiles at Karly and puts her arm around her briefly. The kids are all quietly listening to the teacher, who is reading a book. Occasionally Karly and Deanne lean into each other, shoulder to shoulder.

Eventually their exchanges carried over into recess, lunch, and choice time. Their first interactions tended to be nonverbal and consisted of hugging or playing with each other's hair. Their initial physical proximity seemed to provide each with security. In an interview with Deanne, I asked her what she and Karly talked about at lunch time:

> "Can you think of things that you and Karly talk about at lunch?"

"Nothing."
"Do you talk about what you've just done, or do you just eat?"
"We just eat. Because we don't want to miss the time" (referring to their scheduled 20 minutes for lunch)!

After a time, Karly and Deanne began playing and talking to each other in ways typical of their age group:

Deanne and Karly are sitting next to each other. Deanne puts her arm around Karly, leans close and whispers to her. She sits up on her feet, hops, and then switches back and forth between feet. She talks with Karly for awhile and this time Karly puts her arm around Deanne. They both try to muffle laughs by putting their hands on their mouths. Deanne talks with Karly again, puts her hand around her and rubs her back. She talks with her some more in a whisper and rubs her head. Karly starts to giggle.

By the spring of their first year together in Caresville, Karly and Deanne were engaging in much longer and extended interactions:

Hand in hand, Karly and Deanne head over to the dress-up area during choice time. The theme is a "tea party." The teachers have set out little tea cups and saucers. Karly and Deanne get dressed in their tea party clothes—long, satiny dresses with feather stoles around their necks. Karly puts on a hat and Deanne wears a long string of pearls. Karly asks Deanne to "sit down" because she is going to be the waitress. She asks Deanne what she would like, "Do you want a cookie or a muffin today?" Deanne responds, "A big sugar cookie!" Karly promptly places an imaginary cookie on the small plate and hands it to Deanne, "Here you are, my dear." "Thank you, my dear," Deanne tells her. They play the whole time at tea party and both groan when the teacher tells them it is time to clean up.

Karly's and Deanne's friendship became established over several months of getting to know one another. For young children, best friends are those they play with the most. Karly and Deanne became friends on that basis. Older children view the process as more complicated. Most believe that friendship is established gradually as they find out about one another's values, interests, and personal characteristics.

Friendships first begin to have some stability when children are around five or six years old, as were Karly and Deanne at the early stages of their relationship. That is, not until this age do children begin to consistently seek out the same child to play with. There is an increase in friendship stability from six to ten years of age, although there is still considerable variation among children. It is not until children are close to 12 years old that the notion of friendship implies an expectation of some kind of permanence. Very long-lasting relationships are not usually characteristic of children's friendships until 16 years of age. At least two factors may account for the increasing stability of friendships at older ages. The first is that children's interests, which lie at the root of many friendships, are less likely to fluctuate as they grow into adolescence. The second is that adolescents, who have developed more sophisticated forms of personal understanding, are able to absorb quarrels without suffering damage to their relationships.

CONTINUATION OF FRIENDSHIP: SETTLING IN

During the continuation phase of a friendship, a relationship is continued with increasing intimacy over an extended period of time (Levinger & Levinger, 1986). In children's friendships, as in those of adults, the changes and growth that occur are seldom obvious. During the spring of their first year together in Caresville, Karly and Deanne had a solid, loving friendship. More often than not they could be found in each other's company. They started off early each school day looking for the other, with Deanne waiting for Karly to arrive from the "special education" school bus. Holding hands, they skipped to class, giggling and chatting. I once asked their teacher what she thought they talked about:

> I think it's stuff all the other girls are whispering
> about, you know—their hair, their clothes, what they
> should do next. It's the same old stuff that all other
> little girls are talking about because we have to ask
> them to be quiet. I think it's all very normal.

Once Karly and Deanne completed the arrival routine, they became busy with class-wide activities and projects. While they seemed comfortable doing these things independently, it wasn't unusual to find them checking in with each other periodically. Although Deanne typically initiated these "check-in" times, on a couple of occasions I observed Karly taking the lead in looking after Deanne, as in the following example:

> One time I was in there and Deanne was supposed to
> be sharing her book with an older child from the sixth
> grade. She seemed really intimidated and nervous
> about the situation. Karly cued into that and stood
> next to Deanne, puting her arm around her and stuff.

Recess was a wonderful time during which Karly and Deanne engaged in many rich, playful, and fun activities. In the beginning of their friendship the two usually played only with each other as in the following example:

> The teacher announced recess and Karly and Deanne
> took off outside holding hands. They played on the
> monkey bars. Deanne swung back and forth and Karly
> usually stayed on one bar to swing. Deanne frequently
> stopped swinging to push Karly or talk to her. Karly
> watched Deanne travel across the bars and clapped for
> her when she made it all the way across.

Eventually their play together at recess carried over from a pair to a small group of girls from their class. The group met regularly for several months during morning and lunch recesses.

The girls often played on the playground equipment and the tire swing:

> Karly left the cafeteria and ran with Deanne, Erin, and
> Sammy to the Big Toy, all holding hands. They ran to
> the tire swing. Karly, Deanne, and Sammy climbed on
> the swing and Erin pushed them for awhile. Sammy
> got off and sat on a log, watching. Karly and Deanne
> swung for awhile. Both were laughing really hard and
> trying to make the swing go faster.

Karly seemed very happy and animated throughout these times, which lasted until the end of Karly's first-grade year and for awhile into the fall of the following school year.

As Karly and Deanne settled into their friendship at school, they began spending time with each other during after-school hours. Karly attended Deanne's sixth and seventh birthday parties. Deanne's mother fondly recalls a tender exchange between the two at Deanne's sixth birthday:

> Deanne had a tea party birthday. All the little girls
> came dressed for tea. Somehow Karly didn't know that
> was what she was supposed to do. So when she came to
> the door without all the attire, Deanne quietly took her
> in her room and helped her find a hat and some
> jewelry. Karly just beamed when she came out.

Karly also had Deanne over to her home for her birthday parties as well as several play dates. While in Caresville one day, Deanne shared her excitement and feelings for Karly:

> The children were seated at tables around the room,
> coloring a picture. Deanne was sitting at a table with
> four girls and a few empty chairs. Karly was sitting
> next to Deanne's left. Deanne talked to the girls about
> her clothes, Karly's birthday party, and what she was
> drawing. The girl sitting across from Deanne said,
> 'Karly's smart.' Deanne looked at Karly and said, "Yeah,
> Karly you are smart." Karly smiled and continued to

color. Deanne said, "My next picture is going to be
about Karly's birthday party."

The significant people in Karly's and Deanne's life realized the value and importance of their friendship, noticing in
particular how ordinary it was. I asked one of their teachers
why she thought the two had connected:

> I think Deanne is shy and hesitant. So at first I
> thought, well, she can latch onto Karly because that's
> a security for her. But then when it developed into a
> friendship, I don't know why or what triggered her
> interest in Karly versus somebody else. Except that
> Karly is fun and funny. I think Deanne gets as much
> out of it as Karly. I don't know if Deanne's all that
> funny, but she will talk about things, get the ball
> rolling, whereas Karly might not. Once it's initiated,
> when I watch them talking, it's not just Deanne
> talking. It's Karly talking back—it's a conversation!

Karly's mother also commented on the importance of
Karly's friendship with Deanne:

> I think she has a wonderful relationship with Deanne.
> Deanne is one of the few children that seems to be
> accepting of her exactly as she is. She doesn't mother
> her. Deanne also has certain expectations in the rela-
> tionship that I think are perfectly normal and healthy.

The growth of friendship is facilitated by the exchange
of intimate information, emotional support, and shared activities. Karly's and Deanne's friendship included all of these
variables at some point. These growth variables (intimacy,
helping, and common activities) seem to lead to increased
benefits and rewards derived from friendship. For example,
as a child becomes more intimate in her relationship with a
friend, she is likely to experience greater rewards from her
friendship by gaining a confidant, who listens to her and cares
about her feelings.

Just as there are variables that help to strengthen a friendship, there are also variables that lead to the breakdown of a friendship. The next section identifies these variables and examines how are they similar to and different from growth variables.

DETERIORATION: DECAY, DUST, AND DIFFERENT NEEDS

Kids may grow apart either geographically or psychologically. Both changes are often beyond children's control. As children grow older, their abilities, interests, and even values change. Friends often develop in a different direction or at a different pace.

During the summer following their first year together in Caresville, Karly and Deanne visited with each other three or four times. With Beth's illness and Deanne's busy family events, however, the girls didn't get together as much as they may have liked. They both continued on in Caresville the following school year, Deanne as a first grader and Karly as a second grader. Observations early in the school year revealed that the girls were maintaining close contact and still engaging in a variety of activities together. Their former "friendship clique" with Erin and Sammy also continued to meet at recess. Karly and Deanne had grown significantly from the previous year both socially and academically. Although Karly still had difficulties with transitions and being self-directed, she was much more verbal and outspoken in class. Deanne had blossomed into a social butterfly. She had many friends and the growth in her self-confidence was sizable.

By winter of that school year Karly and Deanne were still interacting with each other frequently, but there was a subtle shift in their relationship. In March, their teacher gave her opinion on the current status of their friendship:

> I think that Karly and Deanne are still good friends,
> but it's less tight. It seemed like in the beginning of the
> year and even to January they were always together.
> Now I feel like Deanne is branching off a bit. I see her

with other kids her age and she has become quite
sought after as a playmate.

The winter also brought cold weather and rain, which meant that the children weren't going outside for recess as often. Eventually the "friendship clique" stopped meeting at the playground and new games replaced old ones. Springtime led to large soccer games on the school fields with many participants coming from Caresville. Deanne was one of the children who played soccer on a regular basis with her peers. Karly, traditionally uncomfortable in large groups and perhaps lacking the confidence or interest to play, began spending her recess time alone or in the company of another classmate, Henry. Henry, whom we will learn about in the next chapter, is a child with mild learning disabilities and poor social skills who also shied away from these large group events.

There was also a change in the way that Karly and Deanne were interacting with each other that spring. More and more frequently Deanne was assuming a directive and helping role in her interactions with Karly. It appeared that she was projecting a sense of responsibility towards her. Two excerpts from observation notes, one during lunch and one during class time, are illustrative of the change:

Karly stood at the lunch table, about three minutes,
not knowing where to go. Deanne (sitting at the table)
called her to come over. Karly just looked. Deanne got
up and brought her over to the table and had her sit
with her. Deanne talked with the girls around her, but
not with Karly. Karly was quiet. When Karly was
finished with her lunch, Deanne reminded her to
throw away her trash.

Karly and Deanne sat at a table with three other
girls. The girls were talking to each other and writing
on their evaluation forms. Karly watched her peers
work. After a couple of minutes Deanne looked over at
Karly's blank paper and reached across the table for a
pencil. She handed the pencil to Karly and said, 'Start

writing.' Karly wrote her name on top of the paper
and then began her self-evaluation. Deanne didn't say
anything else to her.

Except for attending each other's birthday parties that year, Karly and Deanne seldom saw each other after school. They did not see each other at all over the summer break. The following school year Karly was assigned to a new third-grade class and Deanne to a second-grade class. The two Caresville teachers moved on to new schools and assignments as well.

The decay of friendship is not simply the breakdown of social exchange. Although it appeared that Karly's and Deanne's friendship had ceased because of moves to new class-rooms and dwindling interest in each other, their friendship had begun to break down prior to that point. One potential reason may be that there was a developmental shift in their social needs and this created too big of a gap between them. Deanne had moved from being an introverted young girl to an outgoing, social child. She had an increased need for expand-ing her relationships and testing her new skills with a variety of peers. Karly, on the other hand, remained most comfortable in the company of one or two children. Karly also seemed to be increasingly aware of her disability and the fact that she was identified by others as different. With this increased aware-ness, Karly seemed to withdraw and limited her interactions to a select number of children. These may have been children with whom she felt "safe." With the withdrawal came passiv-ity on Karly's part. Perhaps Deanne became impatient with Karly and felt frustrated with Karly's lack of social progress, when her own social growth was so evident.

The reasons children give for decay of a friendship in-clude statements regarding such characteristics as disloyalty and phoniness and comments that have a moralistic overtone. Some relationships withstand moves, others break apart. An-other possible cause of breakdown in friendship may be differ-ences in the rate of social development of members of the pair. This was more likely the case for the decay of the friendship between Karly and Deanne. Just as one grows out of a pair of shoes, Deanne may have simply grown out of her friendship with Karly.

ENDING: MOVING OUT

In most cases, losing friends is a stressful experience for children. Children's relationships are rarely disrupted permanently by a single argument. Rather, the breakups are likely to be the final result of a gradual drifting apart, set in motion by one or both friends' increasing recognition that they no longer provide the same satisfaction to one another (Rubin, 1980). The endings of friendships and their replacement with new ones should usually be taken as signs of normal development rather than of social inadequacy. Even Dr. Benjamin Spock supports the loss of friends as a positive experience in the growth of a child: "The very fact that friendships wax and wane is evidence that at each phase of growth children are apt to need something different from their friends, and, therefore have to find a new one from time to time."

Friendship endings are seldom completely mutual. One child typically becomes disenchanted with the relationship sooner than the other and becomes the "breaker-upper." As they approach adolescence, children sometimes become intensely preoccupied with the status of their friendships, as if to prepare themselves for the endings that will eventually take place (Rubin, 1980). More generally, the ending of a close friendship, whether because of physical separation or psychological disengagement, usually represents a crisis of some proportion in the child's life. Parents often seem to underestimate the importance of these losses, especially when they are dealing with younger children.

By the time that Karly and Deanne had moved on to their new classrooms, their friendship was over. Even though there were opportunities for them to interact during shared recess times and lunch, they did not. This was not surprising given that the classroom environment is typically where young children build and maintain their friendships. Physical proximity remains an important factor not only in the selection of friends, but also in determining whom a young child chooses to play with. Most children in the primary grades and quite a few in the intermediate grades select their classmates as friends. When a friend is no longer in the same class, it is not unusual for the friendship to eventually lose its steam and die out all together. Approximately six months after Deanne and Karly had moved on to new classrooms, I asked Deanne about Karly and whether they saw each other socially. Her response was matter of fact:

> "Do you see Karly at all this year?"
> "No. She's not in my class anymore."
> "Do you see her after school or on the weekends?"
> "No. She doesn't live in my neighborhood. She's far away."

Conclusion

Karly's and Deanne's friendship progressed through many of the stages most children experience in a friendship. While their story did not necessarily end happily, it was typical of what children at this age encounter. Perhaps the most striking aspect of their story was how ordinary their friendship was. As the previous chapter brought out and as the following chapters will show, disability is an important feature and characteristic of the other friendships studied. Disability was not a matter of significance in Karly's and Deanne's friendship. While Deanne was aware that Karly was different, it did not affect her feelings for Karly or her behavior toward her. Deanne treated Karly as she might any other friend. Likewise, Karly responded to Deanne in the same way. I asked Deanne's mother about her perception with regard to this issue:

> I think that Deanne knows Karly has a disability. The only comment that I ever heard her say about it was when somebody would ask Karly if she had a disability and Karly would say, "no." Deanne would laugh at that

and say, "Karly doesn't think she has a disability. But she
does." While she's obviously aware of it or at least aware
of the terminology—to what extent she understands? I
don't know. Not a very deep awareness anyway.

Karly's and Deanne's story provides insight to our understanding of friendship between two children, one with a
disability and one without, attending an inclusive school setting. First and most importantly, Karly's and Deanne's relationship showed something exciting: a child with a significant
disability can experience a typical friendship that is rewarding and mutually beneficial. Second, their friendship under-
scored that context, attitude, and personal value is critical to
the fostering of such relationships. The Caresville teachers
promoted social relationships between children and designed
activities that allowed children to interact cooperatively and
be responsible for each other. The teachers valued all of their
students. Karly was an integral member of the Caresville community. Without this sense of belonging, it is unlikely that she
would have been able to make friends in that community. Her
teachers, as well as her parents, insisted that Karly receive
any related special services such as physical therapy or academic assistance within the classroom. They were concerned
that if she was "pulled out" of the classroom, this would be
stigmatizing and counterproductive to the sense of community in Caresville. Finally, Karly's and Deanne's parents respected the significance of this friendship to each. Karly's
mother was thrilled that Karly had a friend who did not mother
her or assume a care-taking role with her. Deanne had the
same expectations for Karly that she would for any other friend.
Likewise, Deanne's parents were happy that their daughter
was engaging in diverse friendships. Even more so, they valued Deanne's relationship with Karly because Karly was sweet,
loving, and kind to Deanne. Karly's and Deanne's families supported their relationship by ensuring that the girls got together
during nonschool times and by making special arrangements
to keep them in touch over vacations and holidays. Since the

girls did not live close to each other, this took effort, planning, and commitment on their part.

Karly's and Deanne's story provides an opportunity to discuss the stages in the life of a friendship and a chance to highlight the importance of having a friend. The next chapter will continue where this chapter ends. As Karly's friendship with Deanne eventually ceased, she began to spend time with Henry, another classmate from Caresville. Their story and others will be used to illustrate how friendships are maintained, what skills are needed to keep a friendship going, and what characteristics make a "best" friend.

References

Epstein, J.L. (1989). The selection of friends: Changes across the grades and in different school environments. In T.J. Berndt & G.W. Ladd (Eds.), *Peer relationships in child development.* New York: John Wiley & Sons.

Levinger, G. & Levinger, A. (1986). The temporal course of close relationships: Some thoughts about the development of children's ties. In W.W. Hartup & Z. Rubin (Eds.), *Relationships and development.* Hillsdale, NJ: Erlbaum.

Rubin, Z. (1980). *Children's friendships.* Cambridge, MA: Harvard University Press.

Chapter 4

Best Friends and the Skills of Friendship

"Love demands infinitely less than friendship."
(George Jean Nathan)

It is a cold October morning, but Ms. Phillips's third-grade class arrives at school eager to begin the week. The children are excited for two reasons. First, they are starting a new project on wetlands this week, which means they will be spending a lot of time outdoors exploring their environment. The children are also excited because Ms. Phillips's quiet enthusiasm and gentle ways make her a favorite teacher among these eight- and nine-year-olds.

The thirty students come in to the classroom, put their coats and backpacks away, and head for their seats. Karly arrives a little late from the special education bus, puts her belongings in their proper space, and goes right to her chair. Ms. Phillips glances over, giving her a quick wink and smile. She is pleased that Karly has learned the morning routine so early in the school year. Karly's hair has grown considerably since last year and it falls down her back in a neatly combed cascade. She has also gotten taller and her body has begun to fill out. She looks like she'll be entering puberty early for her age. She now dresses with a greater flair for coordination among colors and styles. She still wears glasses and has somewhat of a bewildered look, however. This morning is no exception. Her mother once said that Mondays are particularly difficult for Karly; it is as if she must relearn the structures and routines of the school week all over. Once settled, Karly makes eye contact with Henry, who sits several seats away from her. Henry smiles shyly in Karly's direction and lets out a quick yawn. His dark hair is still wet from the morning comb down. His polo shirt is red and looks bright against his khaki-colored jeans. Henry stifles another yawn as he fumbles in his desk for a paper and pencil.

As the class quiets down, Ms. Phillips shares the day's schedule with her students and begins a discussion on poetry. She tells them that they will spend the first part of this morning reading and writing poems. She asks, by show of hands, who will be writing poems. Four children raise their hands. Then she asks who will be reading poetry. The rest of the group, including Karly and Henry, put their hands high in the air. Ms. Phillips excuses the students to find their poems and begin.

Karly stands next to her seat and watches her classmates move around. Then Henry walks across the room to Karly and picks up her hand. They do not speak. Ms. Phillips asks if they are going to read poetry together. They nod and move away, still holding hands. Ms. Phillips tells them, "You go, Henry, and Karly will follow, but you don't need to hold hands." They drop hands, find a poetry book from the bookcase, and sit close together in the carpeted reading area. They take turns reading to each other and they chat about the pictures. Karly is a much better reader than Henry and although she speaks very softly, her articulation is clearer. Henry struggles with his articulation during his turn and gets flustered with some of the unfamiliar words. But Karly gently helps him sound them out and she doesn't dwell on his stumbling recitation. In contrast, Henry vocally compliments Karly's reading. He encourages her to continue when she hesitates, occasionally patting her on the back.

After the poetry reading Karly and Henry will continue on with the school day spending recess, lunch, and as many academic activities together as they can. Although they played together in Caresville the prior year, they did not become "best friends" until this fall in third grade. Ms. Phillips occasionally voices her concern that they are inseparable but justifies this behavior by comparing it to others' in her class. Most third graders have a best friend and constant companion who is usually from the same class. Karly's and Henry's "best" friendship is also an extremely important aspect of each of their lives.

The Importance of Best Friends

The presence of even one close friend in a child's life is extremely important to his sense of self, his ability to get along with others in his adult life, and his happiness and sense of belonging. Furthermore, researchers find that children without best friends are lonelier than children with best friends, regardless of how well-accepted they are by their peer group (Parker & Asher, 1989; 1993b). A best friend is someone a child counts on to provide comfort in times of sadness, to provide companionship at recess and lunch times in school, and to listen and respond to doubts, insecurities, fears, and accomplishments. The world is considerably less scary when we have a companion to face it with. When a child begins kindergarten or moves from one school to another, the most significant and memorable event he will likely experience will be making a new friend. Because most adults can recall vividly the impact having a friend made on their own childhood, many parents and teachers are sensitive to the child who does not have a friend. There are good reasons, as will be discussed in Chapter 7, to worry about these children.

Not only does a best friend help a child develop a sense of security and support, but interactions with close friends provide many lessons that enhance a child's development of self-concept and beliefs about his abilities. Friends teach numerous life skills, such as how to really get by in school; the art of insults; the sort of pranks that are fun for everyone; the kinds of mischief that are enjoyable and not too harshly punished; and where lines can and should be drawn (Duck, 1991). Friendships teach children social skills; interpersonal competence (how to handle people without too much conflict); the ability to communicate skillfully and persuasively; and relational competence (the skill of handling matters such as intimacy, privacy, and trust in a mature manner). Perhaps the most significant aspect of having "best" friendships in childhood is that they will clearly shape later adult relationships and the child's ultimate willingness to engage in them (Duck, 1991).

WHAT IS A BEST FRIEND?
DEVELOPMENTAL DIFFERENCES

What makes a best friend? The answer depends somewhat on a child's developmental age, although certain characteristics are present at all ages. Researchers, using child interviews, parent and teacher questionnaires, and direct observations, generally agree on three main conditions that mark these friendships (Bukowski, Newcomb, & Hartup, 1996, p. 3):

1. Reciprocities or equivalencies in the "benefits" that are derived from the social exchanges between two friends;
2. Liking to spend more time with one another than with others; and
3. Affection and having fun.

Even young children have some sense of the significance of referring to another as their "best friend." Using the phrase

"She's my best friend" or "You're my best friend" lends them an air of self-importance. Young children may even wield these phrases as a means of power or control. For example, it is not uncommon to hear three- and four-year-olds say, "If you don't share this toy (or anything for that matter) I won't be your best friend!" For young children, best friends are often transient and quickly replaced. Children ages three to five characteristically view best friends as "momentary playmates" or whomever they are playing with at a given time. At this age children do not have a clear understanding of an enduring relationship that exists apart from specific encounters with another person. Their interactions with friends often include both fighting and cooperation. Friendships dissolve easily during play due to the egocentric nature of the preschooler's interactive styles. Just as quickly as old friendships dissolve, new friendships are established.

By six years of age children begin to understand that cooperation and reciprocity are important to friendships. Unlike very young children, whose best friends are their parents, family pets, siblings, or anyone else they happen to be with, the six-year-old's best friends are more likely same-age peers. Friends become very important to the six-year-old's quality of life and he enjoys spending time with his friends. Nonetheless, friendships still come apart easily. The alternation between arguing and cooperating is typical of this stage and it helps children learn that resolving differences is part of having a close relationship. At this age children carry the expectation that "best friends" spend more time with one another than "ordinary friends" or acquaintances. Best friends are also someone with whom to share positive interactions and toys or snacks.

As children grow in their awareness of themselves and others there are changes in what they need from, and contribute to, friendships. While young children associate friendship with sharing of material goods and participating in fun activities, older children feel that friendship involves sharing private thoughts and feelings out of mutual respect and affection (Youniss & Volpe, 1978). Gessel and Iig (1949), pioneers in research on childhood friendships, found that true "best friend" relationships appear at around eight or nine years. At this stage friendships become more stable and they do not dissolve easily. There is reciprocity now and children maintain their friendships in spite of occasional conflicts.

It took Karly and Henry a couple of years to be seen as best friends by their parents and teachers. Karly's friendship with Deanne had slowly deteriorated during her second-grade year. It wasn't uncommon then to find Karly by herself during recess and lunch. Deanne had made new friends and had established closer ties with old ones. Although she still spoke of Karly affectionately, they didn't seem to provide each other with reciprocal benefits to maintain their friendship.

While Karly was often observed alone at recess that spring, she was having an increasing number of social interactions with Henry in their Caresville classroom. Karly and Henry first became acquainted because they attended speech therapy together for 45 minutes, two times a week. Although Karly and Henry both had IEPs, speech therapy was the only time that they were not included with the rest of their classmates. Therapy took place in a small office on the other side of the school building. Twice a week one of the Caresville teachers would remind Karly and Henry that it was time to go to "group." Henry, more often than not, would approach Karly, take her hand, and lead her to the therapy room. Karly would reluctantly follow, confused by the change in her routine. Once in the speech room the communication specialist engaged Karly and Henry in numerous activities to practice their articulation and communication skills. The specialist used the children's personal experiences and ideas to guide their language development. These sessions gave Karly and Henry the opportunity to get to know each other.

Unlike Deanne's and Karly's friendship, which had grown out of natural exchanges initiated by both children, Henry initiated the early social interactions with Karly, as illustrated in the following:

*The children in Caresville were working in groups of
two to four on an art project. Karly walked around a
bit, then sat on the ground a few feet away from two
other children. Henry sat down next to her. He placed
three cardboard toilet paper tubes and a piece of tin
foil in her lap. He got up and walked to a table to get
more supplies. When he returned he sat back down
next to Karly and began work. Karly watched for a
moment and then started on her project.*

After awhile, Henry began to seek out Karly at recess and
lunch times as well. Generally he found Karly alone on the
Big Toy, the wooden apparatus made up of several ladders, a
slide, and a tire swing where Karly and Deanne had played
many times before:

*Karly stood alone next to the Big Toy. Henry arrived a
couple of minutes later and climbed to the top ladder.
He kindly asked her if she needed help to climb up. She
shook her head 'no.' She didn't climb but sat on the
bottom of the Big Toy. Henry climbed down and sat
next to her. They didn't say much. When the bell rang
signaling the end of recess, Karly and Henry walked
quietly side by side to class.*

After a couple of weeks of Henry's gentle prodding, Karly
opened up and seemed to enjoy these exchanges with Henry:

*Karly and Henry walked over to the Big Toy area. They
were both wearing shorts on this hot day. Karly went
to a bar and draped one leg over it. She was trying
really hard to get up. Henry gave her a little boost. She
made it! She gave Henry a shy smile and he joined her.
They both sat on top of the apparatus. Occasionally
Henry yelled down at someone passing by using a silly
voice. Karly laughed and giggled at him. When the bell
rang, Henry verbally guided Karly down using a gentle,
yet authoritative tone of voice.*

There are probably several reasons why Henry chose friendship with Karly. First, in speech therapy, he was able to enjoy a side of Karly that few others did. She was talkative, funny, and open. These were traits that she shared with children she knew well and felt safe with, as she had with Deanne. Furthermore, Karly was an easy friend to be with. Henry got to make the majority of the decisions about what activities they would do. Henry, a child challenged by poor speech articulation and learning disabilities, didn't feel confident around too many children. Because Karly was so accepting of him, he had the rare opportunity to be in control of a relationship. Their personalities were well suited to each other. Karly was also a safe, nonthreatening person. She did not make fun of Henry and she kept his secrets to herself.

On the other hand, their relationship was also positive for Karly. Henry grew very protective of Karly. For example, he did not allow other children to enter into their play if they might be rough or scary to Karly. If they were on the Big Toy together and other children who appeared threatening approached, Henry would discreetly suggest to Karly that they play somewhere else and guided her there. In addition to keeping her safe, Henry showed pride in Karly's accomplishments and encouraged her to do her best work. Because both had academic delays, they were frequently paired together in their third-grade class. I asked their teacher, Ms. Phillips, "Do Karly and Henry choose each other as partners often?" She replied, "They always choose each other as partners. And it has worked out pretty well for other kids in the class because they are usually well-matched. Occasionally Karly is paired with other kids and so is Henry. But usually they are together."

After several months together, their relationship seemed to be more equal. As one observer close to the two children noted: "Henry's and Karly's friendship appears stronger this year [third grade]. Karly seems to enjoy Henry more and he seems to respect her more, letting her do things on her own. They have eaten lunch together every day this year and are always together at recess." At this point, Karly's and Henry's relationship met the three conditions noted earlier that are characteristic of "best friends." First, each was receiving reciprocal benefits. Henry received acceptance, feelings of control, and the opportunity to interact with someone who helped him feel better about himself. Whenever Henry was asked to describe his relationship with Karly, he mentioned helping her, something of which he was quite proud. Karly also benefited from her friendship with Henry. Henry provided companionship, safety, and humor. Second, they clearly liked to spend their time together, rather than with other children. Finally, there were many expressions of affection and plenty of fun:

> Henry and Karly sat together at an electronic keyboard. Henry looked at Karly and laughed. Karly smiled back at him. He played the keyboard and she put her hand over his and they played and laughed. They continued to hold each other's hands and play with the keyboard. Henry sang to Karly as he played and Karly hummed along quietly, but happily.

WHAT DO CHILDREN EXPECT OF THEIR BEST FRIENDS? DEVELOPMENTAL DIFFERENCES

In each of the pairs of friends I studied, the children had underlying expectations as to what they hoped to receive from their friendship. For example, Henry and Karly both expected that the other would provide companionship, trust, and a sense of commitment to the relationship.

How did the expectations of these seven pairs of friends compare with the expectations of children who do not have disabilities? To answer this question, I turned to a study in which two researchers asked Canadian children in grades one through eight to write an essay about what they expect of their best friends that is different from what they expect of people who are not best friends (Bigelow & La Gaipa, 1975). The researchers found three stages of development that correlated with the participants' ages among the responses:

1. Common activities, looking for similarities in others, and propinquity (proximity);
2. character admiration; and,
3. acceptance, loyalty, and commitment; genuineness, common interests, and intimacy potential.

They found that first and second graders expected their best friends to engage in the same activities and to be close by if they needed them (Stage 1). They also noticed that during the second and third grades there was a reward-cost stage in which the children appeared to weigh the cost of their efforts to make or maintain a friendship to the possible gains from the relationship. Fourth and fifth graders expected their best friends to share the same values, rules, and sanctions (Stage 2). The issue of fairness, as well as loyalty to the relationship, was an underlying component of their friendships. During the third stage, found typically among sixth, seventh, and eighth graders, self-disclosure, intimacy, and personality types were critical factors in differentiating best friends from other friends (Bigelow, 1977).

Both third graders, Karly and Henry felt they were best friends because they cared about each other and they showed an awareness of how their actions affected the feelings of the other. They also had traits that were pleasing to the other. Character admiration, or liking the specific personal characteristics that a child displays, is something that children Karly's and Henry's age typically look for in a relationship (Bigelow, 1977). These characteristics are fairly straightforward for the nine-year-old, who tends to value kindness, politeness, the act of sharing, and the lack of aggressive tendencies in his friends. Children this age also look for similarities in personalities among their peers (Epstein, 1989). Three other pairs of friends profiled in this book also illustrate friendships that were built on the basis of character admiration and finding shared similarities. For Nelle and Theresa and Corrie and Lindsey, the similarities shared were isolation and a need for companionship. For Aaron and Cole, the common thread was humor.

I once asked Theresa, a typically developing sixth grader, how she became friends with Nelle, a sixth-grade student who was nonverbal and had moderate developmental delays. Theresa shared the story of their first meeting:

> I had friends in third grade but they weren't really very nice to me and so I really didn't have anybody to be my friend. Nelle was new at school that year and she was usually by herself at recess. I saw her and decided I would play with her. She looked really nice and I didn't think she would be mean to me.

Nelle's "niceness" was an important character trait for Theresa. Theresa felt safe and comfortable in Nelle's presence and she didn't worry about being emotionally wounded by her. Theresa also identified with Nelle. She saw someone else who was in need of a friend. Finally, being friends with Nelle gave Theresa the opportunity to express her caring, nurturing side. Theresa's mother shared her perception of her daughter's need at that time:

> I think Theresa has this need to reach out and to help and that makes her feel good that she was doing that. But I don't think that is the only reason she's with Nelle. Theresa likes Nelle and enjoys being with her and they have fun.

The friendship between Nelle and Theresa is described more fully in Chapter 8.

Another relationship that arose out of a joint need for companionship was the one between Lindsey and Corrie. Lindsey, a fourth-grade girl who experiences mild learning disabilities, became friends with Corrie, a fifth-grade girl with moderate developmental delays, when they were placed in the same third- and fourth-grade multi-age classroom together. Lindsey, who has a long history of moving to different schools, was new to Jane Austen school that year. Unlike Theresa, Lindsey did not deliberately seek Corrie out. Rather, a special education aide noticed that the two always ate lunch alone and one day asked Lindsey if she would like to move and sit next to Corrie. Lindsey's response was telling of her poor self-esteem. She replied: "It's okay. Corrie doesn't have to talk to me if she doesn't want to. I don't have to sit next to her if she doesn't like it." The aide convinced Lindsey that she would be helping Corrie out by providing her with a friend at lunch, and from that day on the two girls ate lunch together every day even after they moved on to different classrooms. Their shared isolation was the bridge that brought these two girls together with the help of a sensitive adult. Their story of friendship and loneliness is presented in Chapter 7.

Like Theresa and Nelle, Aaron and Cole also became friends while they were in third grade together. Unlike Theresa and Nelle and Corrie and Lindsey, Aaron and Cole were not shy, lonely children who needed companionship. What they shared was a sense of humor and the delight in having fun. When Aaron, a typically developing sixth grader, talked about his friendship with Cole, a child with severe disabilities, he spoke about the fun they had together. Aaron's mother recognized the common bond that these two boys shared: "Aaron tells me, 'he's [Cole's] funny, mom, and he has humor.' And Cole is funny—I've seen that. Aaron's a joker too. So they have similar personalities in this way." Aaron's and Cole's story is further profiled in the next chapter.

By the time they reach adolescence, children view loyalty and commitment as essential qualities in a best friend. Friendship formation becomes marked by greater emotional intensity, closer interactions, increased tolerance of conflict, and added stability. Many adults can probably think of at least one long-lasting friendship that developed during their early teenage years because these characteristics were in place. Children at this later stage regard friendship as a relationship that takes shape over time. Friends are seen as providers of intimacy and support. Adolescents also realize that best friends need to be psychologically compatible, to share interests, and to have mutually agreeable personalities.

Molly's and Stacy's friendship is one example of a relationship that began in childhood and survived the changes of early adolescence, even though the girls experienced a shift in their friendship that was brought on by differing interests and developmental levels. In sixth grade, Stacy explained how her relationship with Molly was different from her friendships with other typically developing sixth-grade girls:

> I think that we're really good friends, but we don't really talk about stuff, like boys and stuff together because I don't think she's [Molly] really into that kind of stuff. But we can talk about other stuff. Sometimes we talk about recess, we talk about stuff that she likes to do. She doesn't really know about the Sonics or Mariners [sports teams] and stuff like that. So we talk about stuff that she knows about and we play together at recess. She likes passing the ball, the tether ball. And if we lower the hoop in our backyard, she can shoot the basketball.

Stacy's mother, when asked about the changes in Stacy's and Molly's friendship from second grade to sixth grade, had this to share:

> I think it's tougher this year because Stacy is getting real mature, I think, for her age. She's a pretty mature kid and Molly, obviously, is not. So their interests are different. Molly wants to go out and play on the Big Toy and slide and play chase. And Stacy wants to look at the boys and giggle with the girls. She's a very social creature. I really wondered what would happen this year, whether they would even have a relationship. But interestingly, they do. They are still very good pals in the classroom and Stacy just loves to take care of Molly. They still talk on the phone and they got together last summer as well as this fall. Even though Stacy is maturing a lot emotionally, she's not leaving Molly behind. She tells me everything Molly does in

school, every single day. She tells me about their
projects, what they presented, and if Molly was absent.

Stacy remained very committed to her friendship with
Molly even though the two were moving along different paths.
When Stacy was in sixth grade and about to graduate, I asked
Stacy's mother, "In your opinion, what continues to drive Stacy's
investment in Molly?" Her response illustrates nicely how Stacy
has moved through the levels of friendship development:

> *It's an investment in a relationship. And I think that is*
> *true of any friend, no matter if they are Molly or if they*
> *are somebody else. If you care about your friends, and*
> *Molly is a friend, then you invest your time, you invest*
> *your emotion, and you invest whatever is necessary to*
> *make the relationship work. So I don't think Stacy's*
> *relationship with Molly is because she's trying to get*
> *anything special out of her, I just think she cares about*
> *her. And Molly cares about Stacy.*

THEORIES ON THE STAGES OF
FRIENDSHIP DEVELOPMENT

According to several social scientists, movement through
the stages of friendship development requires three levels of
social understanding. First, there is progression in a child's
ability to take another person's view. Initially, children view
friendship in a one-sided and egocentric way—what can a friend
do for me? Only at later stages do children become capable of
standing back and taking the other person's viewpoint. Second, there is a shift from viewing people in the physical sense
to viewing them psychologically as well. Children begin to
empathize and to try to determine what their friends are feeling and then act accordingly. Finally, children's ideas of friendship change from momentary interactions to social systems
that endure over a period of time. The child realizes that he
can count on his best friends over the long haul.

Among the friendships I studied, the one between Karly and Henry perhaps best showed this progression. While Karly's and Henry's friendship began as a series of temporary interactions, it developed into a relationship where both understood the other's feelings and provided comfort when necessary. They also began to anticipate seeing each other. On the few occasions that either was absent from school, it was clear that they missed their friend and felt displaced for that day. Their friendship had become a source of social support.

Many developmental psychologists believe that children work out for themselves what friendships are all about on the basis of their social exchanges with others. Through their interactions with peers, children discover that other children are similar to them in some ways and different in others. Eventually children make sense of what they have learned about others, which leads to a more sophisticated understanding of friendships in general. Accordingly, these developmental psychologists believe that the growth of social understanding depends on developing intellectual skills and on having numerous and varied social experiences (Duck, 1991). For example, talking openly about conflicts may be one valuable way to further a child's understanding of friendship because it engages both intellectual skills and actual experience. Children of all ages need skills in sharing and cooperation to make friends, but older children require skills in identifying shared interests, disclosing thoughts and feelings, and maintaining an atmosphere of trust.

Theories on the Skills of Friendship

From early childhood through adolescence, children acquire a range of friendship skills. Steve Duck (1991), who has studied relationships for two decades, emphasizes the importance of planning and providing structure when thinking about the development of friendship skills: "Friendship making ability is absolutely not instinctive or genetically programmed, nor is it something that is inherited. Rather it is something that comes through and in the social experiences of childhood and adolescence. It is something that has to be acquired, learned carefully and practiced" (p. 134). The inability of some children to make friends transcends race, sex, and class, as well as the presence or absence of a disability. Dr. Duck believes that making friends is "a lesson that some people learn well, some grasp with difficulty for eventual success, and some learn so poorly that it afflicts their adult relationships with a virulent social canker" (Duck, 1991, p. 135).

Child developmental researchers, James Youniss and John Volpe (1978), asked children of various ages what actions were necessary to make or keep friends. They found that younger children associated friendship with sharing material goods or doing fun activities together, while older children reported the importance of sharing private thoughts and feelings out of a sense of mutual respect and affection. Youniss stressed that with development comes an increased understanding of the interrelationship between interpersonal and personal psychological states. For example, older children more clearly understand that an act of friendship can transform a lonely or sad person into a happy one.

What, then, are some of the skills required to make a friend? According to experts in this field, children must be able to feel and express intimacy, respect others' rights, cooperate, keep and share secrets, help others, enter into others' play, resolve and manage conflict, and become accepted by their peers. Furthermore, children need a reasonable level of self-esteem, an understanding of fairness and cooperation, the ability to recognize activities that suit a particular level and style of a relationship, trust, self-disclosure, and the ability to reciprocate! These skills seem daunting for even the most socially mature child, but what about for children who may not possess the verbal abilities or comprehension to develop or use these skills? Are close friendships with others possible for children who may be lacking in some of these areas? Maybe a better question to ask is, when children do not have the traditional friendship-making skills, do they have other qualities or abilities that may appeal to potential friends instead?

Christine Hurley-Geffner (1995) has carefully considered the issue of friendships for children with developmental disabilities. She has found that there are four problems that make it difficult to answer these questions definitively at present. She has found:

1. Limited opportunities for children with developmental disabilities to interact with their typically developing peers;
2. Too much emphasis on the development of social skills;
3. Too much emphasis on remediating the "deficits" of the child with the disabilities;
4. Failing to acknowledge the capabilities of children with developmental disabilities, including those children who are often defined by their social difficulties (p. 109).

Clearly, these societal problems make it difficult for many children with disabilities to learn and practice friendship skills. This, in turn, makes it difficult to assess the potential of these children for forming true friendships with their nondisabled peers. Fortunately, however, the four problems listed above may not be so difficult to address. For instance, children with disabilities are increasingly being given opportunities to interact with typically developing peers when they attend inclusive schools and extra curricular events. Secondly, parents and professionals are learning how to create environments that are caring and supportive of the development of friendships. Indeed, the last section of this book is dedicated to that goal. The emphasis on facilitating and supporting positive interactions between children, rather than focusing only on their social skills or deficits, will hopefully broaden a child's opportunities to make friends. Finally, as the seven pairs of friends studied in this book reveal, mutual benefits *are* being found in at least some friendships involving children with and without special needs. Henry's and Karly's friendship is a good case in point. I once asked one of the Caresville teachers why she referred to Henry's and Karly's relationship as a "true friendship." Following is her response:

> I think it's the give and take. That it is not all one-sided. Their friendship is based on common interests, common enjoyment, and that Karly might be comforting to Henry and vice versa. There's a connection there and it's not, "I'm going to be kind to Karly because she's special." In Caresville we have worked really hard on making it more of a natural thing—that all children are part of our community and they are friends and they have good things about them and maybe things we wish were different but we're all part of a family.

Conclusion

Having at least one best friend can make a great difference in a person's life. It is usually with our best friends that we can be most like ourselves. Best friends provide comfort, companionship, and an outlet for expressing intimate and closely guarded thoughts and feelings. There is developmental progression in children's ideas about best friendships, with joint activities and proximity characteristic of preschool and early childhood friendships; conformity and cooperation marking friendships in middle childhood and loyalty; mutuality and intimacy serving as common threads in preadolescent and adolescent friendships. Harry Stack Sullivan (1953), one of the first theorists in this area, sums it up this way: "If you look very closely at one of your children when he finally finds a chum, you will discover something very different in the relationship—namely, that your child begins to develop a new sensitivity to what matters in another person. And this is not in the sense of 'what should I do to get what I want,' but instead 'what should I do to contribute to the happiness or to support the prestige and feelings of worthwhileness of my chum'" (p. 52).

Sometimes the benefits of a reciprocal relationship are simple. For example, Karly and Henry experienced a feeling of joy and contentment while in each other's company. When I asked Henry a couple of years ago about his friendship with Karly, he was a bit baffled by why it might be an important question to address:

Me: Henry, why do you like to play with Karly?

Henry: Well we play together!

Me: Okay, what type of play? What do you do when you play?

Henry: Well, we play at recess. We go to different things like "Fun World."

Me: What's "Fun World?"

Henry: You know. It's just make believe.

Me: Okay. So what do you do at Fun World?

Henry: Well, it was built about a thousand years ago. Karly and me like it there. Sometimes we act like we're going to a place to win a boat or a car or something. We make believe that we win. It's fun.

Henry's matter-of-fact response was understandable. The companionship and happiness Henry and Karly received from each other was obvious. However, the benefits for some of the other friends discussed elsewhere in this book were not so evident. In the next chapter the issue of reciprocity will be more fully explored as we learn more about the benefits that children, both with and without disabilities, gain from their friendship with another. An understanding of all potential benefits will help lay the groundwork for later chapters on creating and facilitating environments that are supportive of all children's friendships.

References

Bigelow, B.J. (1977). Children's friendship expectations: A cognitive-developmental study. *Child Development, 48,* 246-253.

Bigelow, B.J. & La Gaipa, J.J. (1975). Children's written descriptions of friendship: A multidimensional analysis. *Developmental Psychology, 11,*105-116.

Bukowski, W.M., Newcomb, A.F., & Hartup, W.W. (1996). *The company they keep: Friendship in childhood and adolescence.* New York, NY: Cambridge University Press.

Duck, S. (1991). *Understanding relationships.* New York: The Guilford Press.

Epstein, J.L. (1989). The selection of friends: Changes across the grades and in different school environments. In T.J. Berndt, & G.W. Ladd (Eds.), *Peer relationships in child development.* New York: John Wiley & Sons.

Gessel, A. & Iig, F.L. (1949). *Child Development.* New York: Harper.

Hurley-Geffner, C.M. (1995). Friendship between children with and without developmental disabilities. In R.L. Koegel & L.K. Koegel (Eds.), *Teaching children with autism* (pp. 105-125). Baltimore, MD: Paul H. Brookes.

Parker, J.G. & Asher, S.R. (1989). Significance of peer relationship problems in childhood. In B. Schneider, G. Attili, J. Nadel, & R. Weissberg (Eds.), *Social competence in developmental perspective* (pp. 5-24). Amsterdam: Kluwer Academic Publishers.

Parker, J.G. & Asher, S.R. (1993b). Friends and friendship quality in middle childhood: Links with peer group acceptance and feelings of loneliness and social dissatisfaction. *Developmental Psychology, 29,* 611-621.

Sullivan, H.S. (1953). *The interpersonal theory of psychiatry.* New York: Norton.

Youniss, J., & Volpe, J. (1978). A relational analysis of children's friendships. In W. Damon (Ed.), *New directions for child development. Vol 1: Social cognition* (pp. 1-22). San Francisco: Jossey-Bass.

Chapter 5

Reciprocity & Rewards:
The Benefits of Friendship for Children with and without Disabilities

"When I give, I give myself."
(Walt Whitman)

For the last half-hour of the school day, Mr. Howard allows his fifth- and sixth-grade students to do whatever they want to do, within reason of course. Some students choose to play games on the computer while others try to complete their homework before the bell rings, leaving their afterschool hours wide open. A lot of the students hang out. They might discuss how the local sports teams are doing or whether so-and-so likes so-and-so. This time each afternoon is relatively calm and controlled, very much like Mr. Howard, who directs his learning environment in a calm, sure manner.

Most afternoons Aaron, a typically developing sixth grader, chooses to spend his free time with Cole, a fellow sixth grader. Cole has severe developmental delays and a serious seizure disorder which is under good control this year. Although he continues to have seizures, they do not leave him listless for hours like they did last year. Cole has limited expressive vocabulary and uses one- or two-word sentences. He does not participate in traditional academic tasks, although he is included with his typically developing schoolmates for the entire school day. Cole has a history of behavioral problems that have ranged from mild noncompliance to adult requests to serious aggressive and destructive behavior such as throwing furniture at others. In spite of his occasional outbursts, however, it is hard not to like him. Cole is like an eager toddler who finds wonder in the world around him. The boys he has befriended in Mr. Howard's class bring him great joy. He appreciates their jokes and harmless teasing. Cole would like nothing better than to hang out with his friends all day, but if he had to choose just one friend, it would be Aaron.

On this unseasonably warm afternoon in late April, Aaron is sitting on the carpeted area with Cole and Nelle, a student with moderate developmental disabilities who also attends Mr. Howard's class as a fifth grader. The three classmates and another typically developing boy have elected to play "Go Fish" during their free time. A special education teaching assistant watches the group from across the room as she helps Mr. Howard with filing.

It is Cole's turn to pick a card. Aaron sits on his knees next to Cole and whispers to Cole to pick one. Cole grabs a stack of cards and Aaron reminds him; "One card, Cole, not all of them." Cole tries again and this time picks a match. Aaron points to the corresponding card in Cole's hand and says, "Put them down on the floor. That is a match, Cole." Cole smiles widely. He looks happily at his growing piles of matched cards.

They continue to play until Mr. Howard asks everyone to clean up and get ready to go home. Nelle and the other boy follow Mr. Howard's request quietly and quickly. Cole doesn't budge. Instead he looks at the ground, breaking eye contact, his form of protest. He is not ready to go home and he doesn't want to stop playing. Aaron calmly cajoles Cole into compliance: "Come on, Cole. You don't want to miss your bus. We can play again tomorrow. I don't want to go home yet either." Cole glances up at Aaron as Aaron hands him his backpack. Aaron gives Cole a gentle tug up and pats him on the back. As he does most afternoons, Aaron will walk Cole to the special education bus before going to his bus. The special education teaching assistant will follow discreetly behind, insuring that Cole gets to the bus safely. Aaron's last words to Cole that day will be, "See ya tomorrow, buddy!" Cole will smile shyly at him and mumble back, "Bye, Aaron."

Aaron and Cole knew each other for several years before becoming friends. Aaron shared with me the story of how he first met Cole:

> Three years ago, well, more than that—four or five
> years ago, I remembered seeing him around school.
> But I never was a really good friend of his then
> because I sat up at the front table and he sat clear to
> the back with some other kids. I saw him once in
> awhile at recess but I didn't know him well. After
> awhile I began to recognize his name and then we
> moved to Howard's class together in fifth grade. We've
> been friends ever since.

During their fifth- and sixth-grade years together, Aaron's relationship with Cole often took on a care-taking tone. Without prompting from adults, Aaron helped Cole with his work, included him at games at recess, and generally watched out for him. Aaron also assumed responsibility for Cole's behavior by explaining to Cole how his actions affected others. The following excerpt from a classroom observation illustrates Aaron's gentle way with Cole:

> Cole was taking Nelle's things out of her bag and
> throwing them on the floor. As soon as Aaron saw, he
> walked right over to Cole and started talking to him.
> He said, "We're making a new rule—no being mean."
> Then he walked with Cole to the front of the room and
> told him to tell another boy what the new rule was.
> Cole tapped the boy's shoulder to tell him but the boy
> walked away. Cole looked confused. Aaron smiled and
> put his hand on Cole's shoulder and told him, "It's
> okay. Just remember the rule." Then he walked Cole
> back to Nelle's stuff and quietly asked Cole to put
> everything back.

In addition to helping Cole learn more appropriate behavior, Aaron provided Cole with companionship, support, and
encouragement, much as any true friend does at this age. A lot
of the time their interactions weren't all that different from
those of typical 11- and 12-year-old boys. I asked Mr. Howard
once, "Do you think Cole's and Aaron's friendship looks different from others' in your class?" Mr. Howard thought for a
moment before responding:

> No, I don't think it looks that different. Well, I was
> going to say one of the differences is that Aaron
> sometimes tells Cole to be quiet, or "Hey Cole, I gotta
> do my work!" But I don't know if that is any different
> than what he might say to Ben leaning over and
> interrupting him. I think I would say that Aaron
> honestly likes Cole and it's not because he's a special-
> needs kid.

Aaron's mother had a different perspective on her son's
relationship with Cole. She focused on Aaron's care-taking tendencies toward Cole: "Aaron's relationship with Cole is almost
a caring, teaching relationship. Like when you first have a baby
and want to show them every new thing in life. I get that feeling
from Aaron, that he wants to let Cole experience all that he has.
I think Aaron gets a joy out of that, I think that is what he likes

to see for Cole." While Cole's friendship with Aaron provided Cole with many benefits including companionship, safety, and his first invitation to a friend's house to play at age 12, the benefits of this relationship were just as evident for Aaron.

Aaron had experienced a lot of angry feelings the past couple of years so it comes as some surprise that his interactions with Cole were gentle, loving, and compassionate. Much of the anger Aaron had was sparked by his fragmented relationship with his father, whom his mother had divorced several years ago. His mother revealed that Aaron and his younger brother have received counseling to talk about some of the anger that they feel toward their father and about the divorce.

When I asked Aaron's mother, Joan, to describe Aaron's relationship with his father, rejection was a common theme. She provided an example. During their sixth-grade year, Cole and Aaron were featured on the cover of the *New York Times* in an article on inclusion and friendships. She shared the article with his grandparents and others and they all commented on how excited they were for Aaron and what a big deal it was for him to be on the cover of such a big newspaper. One weekend, when Aaron was going to visit his father, his mother gave him a copy of the paper to share and Aaron asked, "What do you think Dad?" His father replied, "Well, that is pretty cool, Aaron. But it's too bad that you had to be on the cover with a picture of Clinton." Joan described this response as typical of Aaron's relationship with his father; that Aaron never quite meets his father's expectations of him.

Mr. Howard described Aaron's struggle with low self-esteem and lack of confidence:

> Aaron I would describe as an underachieving student who, while not completely isolated, has some social difficulties. But he does have some friends and he knows how to interact. He wouldn't be one of the most popular boys or girls in the room. He can be pretty outspoken if you ask him to be. But he generally keeps somewhat reserved and he's reluctant to keep up on work. He slid a great deal academically last year,

> *almost as if he was just going to give up. He exhibited*
> *very little confidence in himself.*

I asked Mr. Howard to describe how he felt Aaron was doing currently, his sixth-grade year: "He's had his best time all year this last term. He has elevated his status and he's responded much more positively to responsibility." Mr. Howard believed that Aaron's relationship with Cole was instrumental in increasing Aaron's self-esteem. He felt that Cole provided Aaron with a leadership role that he usually didn't take with his other classmates: "So, he gets that place, Aaron has that place, because of the attention that the inclusive schooling's got. It's like, 'yeah, I am this important person. I don't see Cole as a special-needs kid, I see him as a friend,' and it's given him a place in my classroom."

The relationship that Aaron and Cole shared had many different layers of meaning. Aaron's friendship with Cole provided him with the opportunity to be a leader, to increase his status in the classroom, and to have his self-esteem elevated at a vulnerable time in his life. From Cole, Aaron also gained unconditional acceptance and trust. While the benefits that their friendship provided for both were different in many ways, they were reciprocal.

Friendship and Reciprocity

Anthony Mannarino has studied the development of children's friendships for many years. He believes that the essential component of friendship, and one that should be included in any definition of the term, is the concept of reciprocity: "Two individuals can be said to have a friendship only if the affection and/or esteem that one expresses toward the other is reciprocated" (Mannarino, 1980, p.46). Mannarino also realizes the difficulty in determining whether the "number and intensity of feelings conveyed by one individual to the other are equally reciprocated"

(p. 46). He suggests that one expects some return of positive regard in order for the friendship to be maintained. In other words, we should not be too quick to describe a relationship as a friendship unless there is evidence of mutual benefits.

One of the recent discoveries in the study of friendships and relationships between people with and without disabilities is that there *are* mutual rewards for both partners in the relationship. The research in this area did not begin, however, by studying mutual benefits. Rather, the professional literature first focused on positive outcomes for just the children and adults with moderate and severe disabilities who had opportunities to interact with nondisabled peers. In the late 1980s and early 1990s, as more children with moderate and severe disabilities were placed in inclusive environments, researchers began to observe the effects of inclusion on nondisabled children and adolescents. It has only been in the past couple of years that we have begun to systematically study the mutual benefits that may occur when children with and without disabilities are friends.

PERCEIVED OUTCOMES FOR CHILDREN AND ADULTS WITH DISABILITIES

The existing research on the benefits and importance of *friendships* for children and adults with disabilities is limited (Guralnick, 1990). However, there is a considerable body of research dating back to the 1980s that highlights the importance of having *social interactions* with typically developing peers for children and adults with moderate and severe disabilities. Some of the most important benefits are summarized below.

In their review of the research on social interactions between children with and without disabilities, Ann Halvorsen and Wayne Sailor (1990) found many studies that showed positive outcomes for children with moderate and severe disabilities when they were educated alongside their typically developing peers. These included:

1. Decreases in rates of inappropriate behavior and increased social initiations in elementary-age students;
2. More positive effect (happier mood and appearance) for children with disabilities who have opportunities to interact with typically developing peers when compared to children with disabilities who do not have these opportunities;
3. Increases in the development and generalization of communication skills, play skills; and social skills;
4. Higher parental expectations for their child's future when their child has an opportunity to interact with typically developing peers;
5. Better chances for more normalized living arrangements and inclusive job opportunities for the future.

These studies revealed the positive impact on children and adults with disabilities who had opportunities to interact with typically developing peers on a wide range of skill areas (i.e., Anderson & Farron-Davis, 1987; Goldstein & Wickstrom, 1986; Hill, Lakin, & Bruininks, 1984; Hunt, Alwell, & Goetz, 1988; Lord & Hopkins, 1986; Murata, 1984; Park & Goetz, 1985; Pumpian, Shepard, & West, 1986; Schactili, 1987; Selby, 1984).

Luanna Voeltz [Meyer] was one of the first researchers in the field to evaluate the attitudes that typically developing children have toward peers with moderate and severe disabilities. She compared the attitudes of typically developing children in grades fourth through sixth across three different groups (Voeltz, 1980, 1982). The first group of students attended schools where there were no students with disabilities ("no contact group"), while the second group of students attended schools that were integrated but did not have a systematic program to support interactions between children with and without disabilities ("low contact group"). The third group of students ("high contact group") attended an integrated school where there was a systematic program to promote positive interactions and attitudes between children with and without disabilities. Dr. Voeltz found that the high contact group had higher acceptance scores toward peers with disabilities than the low contact group, which had higher scores than the no contact group. These studies helped push forward a line of intervention research that promoted the social interactions and relationships between children with and without disabilities. Researchers and educators have found that increased interactions between children with and without disabilities are associated with many benefits for children with disabilities and positive attitudes for the nondisabled children toward people with disabilities. But are there actual *benefits* for the typically developing child or adolescent who has a relationship with a peer with disabilities?

PERCEIVED OUTCOMES FOR NONDISABLED CHILDREN AND ADOLESCENTS

Although the rationale for placing children with disabilities in general education environments is based on values and practices that are relevant to the needs of *all* students (Sapon-Shevin, 1990), until recently, very few studies focused on describing and analyzing the experiences of typically developing children and adolescents who attended inclusive environments. One of the first and richest accounts of these experiences was reported by Carola Murray-Seegert (1989), who conducted a year-long ethnographic study of social relations between high school-aged students with severe disabilities and typically developing peers who served as their tutors. She found that the motivation for the typically developing students engaged in relationships with their schoolmates with disabilities went beyond what she termed "helping the handicapped." The typically developing students she came to know described themselves as benefiting from their experience in several ways: learning from the students with disabilities, having the positive experience of supporting another person, and increasing their ability to deal with disabilities they may face in their own lives. She attributed these perceived benefits to the opportunity these students had to assume responsibility for another person, something she feels has been missing in the cultural context of modern U.S. society.

Douglas Biklen, Cathleen Corrigan, and Deborah Quick (1989) reported additional benefits. They interviewed typically developing elementary-aged children who were involved in one of the first demonstrations of inclusive schooling in Syracuse, New York, about their perceptions of people with disabilities. The children described benefits in three areas: 1) learning to interpret differences in appearance and behavior in new ways; 2) making connections between the feelings of children with disabilities and their own experiences; and 3) seeing each other's worth. Overall, the researchers felt that their study confirmed that children of "widely varying abilities can come to accept, appreciate and interact with each other" (p. 219). They also found that the nature of the school setting and teachers' strategies greatly influenced the effective interactions between the children with and without disabilities.

Charles Peck, Jodi Donaldson, and Michele Pezzoli (1990) reported similar findings to the ones above following interviews with high school-aged students who had developed personal relationships with students with severe disabilities when they served as their tutors. They found six categories or types of benefits for the 21 typically developing students they interviewed. First, many of the students made comments indicating growth in their understanding and appreciation of their personal characteristics. The researchers called this category "self-concept." Responses found in this category included, "I felt good about myself," and "I learned who I was." The second type of benefit found was titled "social cognition," and referred to students' increased understanding of the feelings underlying the behavior of their schoolmates with disabilities (e.g., "they have feelings, too, and they need to have the same things we do") and of human differences (e.g., "he was coming from a completely different world, which was good, because

I learned a lot and he learned a lot"). The third and fourth types of benefits found were reduced fear of human differences (e.g., ". . . you get to meet a whole range of people—so you're not so afraid of the unknown anymore") and tolerance of other people (e.g., "I've treated my own friends better. . . I haven't been as cold to people"). The fifth category was development of personal principles. That is, Peck and his colleagues found that the typically developing students interviewed made comments that reflected "further formation, clarification or commitment to personal, moral, and ethical principles" (p. 244). Finally, the sixth category of benefits and the one likely to be most mutually rewarding for both the students with and without disabilities was "relaxed and accepting friendships." Students made comments on the value of the personal acceptance they perceived from their peers with disabilities and they commented on the relaxed nature of the interactions (e.g., "I felt like I could just be myself and have fun").

While the three studies described above suggested many possible benefits for nondisabled children and adolescents engaged in relationships with peers with moderate and/or severe disabilities, they were focused on a limited number of settings. Furthermore, the settings where the studies were conducted were considered to be model demonstration sites for inclusion and integration efforts. Researchers were concerned about whether there would be similar findings at sites where there were less intensive supports for inclusion. In an effort to address these issues, two studies were conducted. First, Charles Peck, Patricia Carlson, and Edwin Helmstetter (1992) conducted a survey study that focused on the perceptions of parents and teachers of students without disabilities enrolled in 44 inclusive preschool and kindergarten programs in Washington state. From the many responses to their survey (125 responses from parents and 95 responses from teachers), the researchers concluded that the survey results were highly consistent with results from the earlier studies. A second study was conducted by Edwin Helmstetter, Charles Peck, and Michael Giangreco (1994). They administered surveys to a statewide sample of nondisabled high school students who had developed relationships with peers with severe disabilities at their high schools. From the 166 responses they analyzed, these researchers found a variety of positive outcomes, including increased feelings of self-worth related to helping others, an increased sense of personal development, and increased tolerance of the behavior and appearance of other people.

A recent study not only confirmed the importance of encouraging social relationships between children with and without disabilities, but also revealed the long-term effects for typically developing children engaged in relationships with peers with disabilities. Gloria Kishi and Luanna Meyer (1994) conducted a study to determine what teenagers report and remember as a result of elementary school experiences involving different levels of social contact with schoolmates with severe disabilities. They gave written questionnaires to 183 typically developing adolescents, who were divided into three groups much like the ones described earlier: a high contact group or social contact group, a low contact group or exposure group, and a no contact group (see Voeltz, 1980, 1982). They also interviewed a subsample of 93 teenagers about their experiences and attitudes toward persons with disabilities and their memories from earlier school experiences. They found that more positive attitudes, more social contact, and more support for full community participation were associated with the high contact group, all of whom had had social contact with peers with disabilities during elementary school. All groups, however, were generally positive in their responses. Their study was significant because it is the only one of its kind to suggest the long-term potential effects for typically developing children and adolescents who develop a relationship with peers with disabilities.

Mutual Benefits: Share and Share Alike

The research summarized above is very positive about the potential benefits typically developing children gain through relationships with peers with moderate or severe disabilities. However, many of the benefits that have been highlighted occurred in studies that cast the nondisabled child in the role of "helper" and the child with disabilities as a recipient of that help. Little research has focused on the reciprocal friendships that develop between children with and without disabilities and the mutual rewards that are experienced. This is perhaps of greater interest to many parents, teachers, and researchers. In fact, the main purpose for writing this book and sharing the seven stories of friendship is to describe what these reciprocal benefits are and to suggest ways that they can be supported and facilitated.

What are the outcomes for children with and without disabilities who are engaged in friendly, mutually based relationships? How are these outcomes similar to and different from the outcomes described for friendships in general? The following sections highlight three main effects that are perceived to be mutually beneficial:

1. warm and caring companionships;
2. increased growth in social cognition and self-concept; and,
3. the development of personal principles and an increased sense of belonging.

COMPANIONSHIP

One of the most important functions of friendship is to enable us to feel safe, loved, and cared for. When researchers asked typically developing children ages 6 to 14 about characteristics that were important to them in a friend, companionship was rated one of the highest on the list (Bigelow, 1977; Bigelow & La Gaipa, 1975). In fact, all seven of the pairs of friends in this book shared a common basis of companionship. Furthermore, three pairs of friendships began due to a need to fill a void, that of not having a companion at school. For instance, when Karly and Deanne first became acquainted in Caresville they each needed a friend. They were both shy, hesitant, and often intimidated by the activity that surrounded them. By becoming friends, they found comfort in each other's presence in an overwhelming situation. Their friendship initially gave them a mutual sense of confidence and security. Once that was established, they were able to engage in fun and playful interactions, typical of their age. One of the Caresville teachers shared her impressions of their companionable relationship:

> Deanne is truly a friend for Karly. They hang out, they comfort each other, they are always hugging and holding hands. Karly and Deanne truly have a "bud" friendship. You don't want to be friends with everyone in the classroom necessarily, but everyone has a need for at least one buddy. That's what they provide to each other.

Theresa's and Nelle's, as well as Corrie's and Lindsey's friendships, also started out when two lonely individuals needed and found companionship, comfort, and security. Both children of the friendship pairs were rewarded by this sense of companionship. Mr. Howard commented on what he felt Nelle, an 11- year-old with moderate mental retardation, received from her relationship with Theresa, a typically developing 11-year-old: "I think Nelle gets her strongest female bond of any situation. Theresa will interact with her, listen to her, and understands her better than anybody else. For Nelle, who does not initiate very much with other kids, it gives her some place, a way to belong to the class" (Staub, Schwartz, Gallucci, & Peck, 1994). Even after Theresa and Nelle moved on to new junior high schools, Theresa felt that she would always remember Nelle as a close friend: "Even though I won't see her very much this year, I still consider Nelle one of my closest friends. I hope to invite her over this summer and write her notes often to keep in touch."

Corrie's and Lindsey's relationship was also built on a common need for companionship. Even though Corrie's and Lindsey's relationship was prompted by an adult, it still provided the same rewards and benefits that Nelle and Theresa and Karly and Deanne received. An adult observer familiar with both girls was asked what she felt the meaning of this friendship was for Lindsey, a 10-year-old girl with mild learning disabilities: "For Lindsey, her relationship with Corrie [a 10-year-old girl with moderate developmental disabilities] is that it means she has a friend. Lindsey has a wall up to protect herself. Corrie is the only one I've seen that she allows in." Even when friendships do not arise from a mutual feeling of loneliness, companionship often becomes an integral part of the relationship.

Stacy and Molly have the longest-lasting friendship of the seven pairs of children in this book. Their friendship began in second grade and has continued into their teenage years. Molly, a pre-adolescent girl with Down syndrome, benefited in many ways from her friendship with Stacy, a typically developing child, as their fifth-grade teacher explained: "I think the strongest relationship is the one between Stacy and Molly. Stacy can quietly affect Molly's behavior in the most positive way, which is done very quietly and respectfully. She gets Molly to do the appropriate thing and instead of acting up, Molly does it."

It might be more difficult for the outsider to determine what benefits Stacy received from her friendship with Molly. Yet their fifth grade teacher, when asked why she thinks their relationship developed, easily puts it into perspective: "Well, they have interacted outside of school too—they go to each other's houses and stuff. I think, though, one of the biggest reasons is respect, and Stacy respects Molly. She doesn't talk down to her, she likes to play with her and she wants to be with her. I think Molly always feels welcome." A special education teaching assistant, close to Molly and Stacy, described what she perceived were the benefits of this friendship for Stacy:

> Stacy benefits from Molly because she can see the growth Molly is making and she realizes she is a big part of the success. She also benefits because Molly makes her feel good—always choosing to sit with her, always goofing around with her.

Karly's and Henry's relationship is perhaps the greatest example of a friendship that was based on mutual rewards of companionship. During their third-grade year the two children were inseparable. They both looked forward to Monday mornings, when they knew they would spend the next six hours together. Their friendship was based on sheer enjoyment of each other's company, a cornerstone of any friendship and one that potentially results in other benefits. Researchers who have studied friendships between typically developing children have found that when children are friendly with others they initiate more interactions with their peers and they interact in more socially mature ways (Doyle, Connolly & Rivest, 1980). Consequently, there may be growth in their ability to understand the feelings and beliefs that underlie the behavior of other people as well as a better understanding of themselves.

GROWTH IN SOCIAL COGNITION AND SELF-CONCEPT

In her year-long ethnographic study in an integrated high school, Carola Murray-Seegert (1989) found that the nondisabled students she studied learned to be more tolerant and patient of others as they become more aware of the needs of their peers with disabilities. The same was true of the participants in Charles Peck's study described earlier (Peck, Donaldson, & Pezzoli, 1990). I too found that several children among the seven pairs of friends I studied became more aware of the needs of others around them. Furthermore, many of the typically developing children became skilled at understanding and reacting to the behaviors of their friend with disabilities.

Aaron, while benefiting from a friendly relationship with Cole, also became skilled at understanding Cole's behavior. As a result, he could help Cole behave more appropriately in classroom and school environments. As Cole became more successful in his abilities, Aaron's self-esteem was boosted. Aaron's mother clearly recognized this benefit for Aaron:

> Our family has recently gone through a tough divorce
> and there are a lot of hurt feelings out there for

> everyone. But at least when Aaron is at school he feels
> good about being there and I think a big reason is
> because he has Cole and he knows that he is an impor-
> tant person in Cole's life.

Likewise, Cole benefited from his friendship with Aaron. Aaron was a trusted friend who was also a role model and mentor for Cole. When Cole felt unsure about the situation around him, he often sought out Aaron for comfort and support. Their sixth grade teacher, Mr. Howard, spoke about this benefit for Cole: "I think that Cole really trusts Aaron and he has a right to trust him because I know that Aaron would never let him down."

Molly's and Stacy's sixth grade teacher, Mr. Page, also felt that Stacy had grown more socially aware as a result of her relationship with Molly. He explained what he thought would be the long-term effects of this relationship for Stacy:

> I think Stacy is at the point where she looks at Molly
> as a friend, and I think inclusion, overall, has ben-
> efited Stacy in the sense that Stacy will never judge
> someone by their mental ability, whether they have
> Down syndrome or are mentally delayed. I think she's
> come to a point where she will look at someone and
> later on in life, if she has a chance to hire someone
> that could do the job with a disability, she would be
> the first one to say "yeah." She would also be compas-
> sionate with that person and understanding, instead
> of demeaning and ridiculing.

Other typically developing students have reported in-creased self-esteem as a result of their friendships with peers with disabilities in not only this work, but others as well (e.g., Peck, et al. 1992; Peck, et al. 1990; Voeltz & Brennan, 1983). Older children who have served as peer tutors or student aides for classmates and peers with disabilities talk about feeling acknowledged and appreciated for helping others. One seventh grade student who was a peer tutor for a classmate with se-vere disabilities made this comment: "It [being a peer tutor] was rewarding. Especially when Kelly [student with disabilities] did something good or made progress. You feel good about yourself because you helped her to do it. I like that" (Staub, Spaulding, Peck, Gallucci, & Schwartz, 1997). The mother of a sixth grade child shared what she perceived her son's experience in an inclusive classroom with a peer with severe disabilities meant to him:

> I think that Patrick [a typically developing 12-year-old boy] has grown a lot. I really think it's been a good maturing experience for him. It has been gratifying for him that he's one of the few kids in the class that seems to be able to handle Sean [classmate with severe disabilities] and deal with him, and his teacher depends on him. I think that is great for the ego, if anything at all, but I know that his self-esteem has definitely increased (Staub, 1995).

The perceived growth in social cognition and self-esteem is not limited to typically developing children. Many of the children with disabilities at Jane Austen also matured socially and improved their social skills as a result of their friendships. Cole learned how to behave in more socially appropriate ways as a result of Aaron letting him know in a respectful manner if he was doing something offensive or immature. Aaron expected Cole to behave like a 12-year-old. Stacy also counted on Molly to act maturely. She quietly modeled appropriate responses for Molly. Since Molly truly respected and admired Stacy as a friend, she would rise to the occasion in order not to embarrass or let Stacy down. For Karly, Nelle, Corrie, and many others, their friendships with typically developing children not only provided them with models for how to socialize appropriately, but also helped them to feel better about themselves. In the presence of their friends, they grew in confidence. This kind of strong sense of one's self is necessary for further growth in many areas, including personal principles, the third outcome area.

DEVELOPMENT OF PERSONAL PRINCIPLES AND A SENSE OF BELONGING

Thomas Berndt (1982) found that typically developing children who are friends have a mutual responsiveness between them that does not occur between nonfriends. He believes that this responsiveness allows for the intimate sharing of thoughts and feelings that contribute to the child's understanding of other people as well as themselves. This increased awareness of others may lead to greater commitment to personal moral and ethical principles, as Peck, et al. (1990) found in interviewing typically developing adolescents who had relationships with peers with severe disabilities. This outcome was also found among the friendships studied here. For example, several of the typically developing children I observed became advocates for their friend with disabilities. In their sixth-grade class, Stacy led a small group of students who were very vocal about making sure that the special education staff did not remove Molly from the classroom to work on skills they believed she could do in the classroom. Because of their concerns, the students in Mr. Page's class asked him to conduct class meetings with Molly present to discuss strategies that would ensure Molly's inclusion in their class. Stacy's personal principles dictated a moral sense of fairness for Molly; that Molly be included as a member of their general education sixth-grade class. As a result of Stacy's advocacy, many of Molly's classmates began to perceive her as a member of their class for the first time:

> Yeah, she's a member of our class. I mean she does everything that everyone else does. She helps in the garden, even though she might not do it as well as other people can. I mean, it's fine. It turns out in the end. She can say that she helped out in the garden and she helped do stuff in our class, because she does a lot of things (quote from Molly's sixth- grade classmate).

Several other typically developing children also developed moral and ethical principles as a result of their friendship with a child with disabilities. As a later chapter will bring out, Theresa struggled with the moral issue of wanting to treat Nelle as she would any friend, not as a recipient of her help. Brittany, a typically developing fifth-grade girl, also struggled with ethical issues in her relationship with Ray, an 11-year-old boy with severe disabilities. Brittany believed that Ray had the right to communicate his needs and protests in the general education classroom, even if Ray's form of communication was loud and disruptive. Because of their moral and ethical commitment to do the "right thing" these children helped ensure and enhance the sense of belonging their friends with disabilities received in their general education classrooms. Membership or a sense of belonging is critical to the development of skills and relationships (Billingsley, Gallucci, Peck, Schwartz, & Staub, 1996). How teachers and other adults can support the outcomes of membership and accompanying benefits will be one of the main topics addressed in Chapter 10.

BEYOND MUTUAL REWARDS: OTHER SPILLOVER EFFECTS

The friendships described in this book not only benefited all the children involved, but many families and parents as well. As part of this research, several parents of the typically developing children were asked about their perceptions regarding inclusion and their child's friendship with a child with disabilities. These parents identified three broad benefits for themselves and their child (Staub, 1995). First, several parents believed that their child had experienced increased awareness and sensitivity toward people with differences. Brittany's mother, for example, observed, "My daughter has gotten to see Ray as a person. She has learned that not all people are the same—that they have different abilities and problems."

Second, some parents noticed growth in their typically developing child's sense of personal principles, including increased patience and more control over their own lives and abilities. Others felt that their child's opportunity to help another person resulted in increased feelings of self-worth that carried over to positive behavior at home. One father of a 12-year-old boy made this comment: "For Kevin, this experience has given him more patience. I think that there is something special between him and Sean [child with severe disabilities]. But I've also noticed that at home he seems more tolerant around his younger brother and sister and even me. Believe me, this is a benefit for me too!"

One of the most exciting and unanticipated findings was that the parents' perceptions about people with disabilities changed too. Many of the parents interviewed shared their regret in not having had experiences similar to their children's. They expressed their wishes that they had gone to school and classes with peers with disabilities because they believed that their own comfort level and feelings regarding people with disabilities would have been drastically different.

Likewise, many parents of children with disabilities perceived that they have benefited from their child's friendship with a typically developing peer. Karly's mother, for example, found great joy in Karly's "ordinary" friendship with Deanne: "I think she has a wonderful relationship with Deanne. Deanne is one of the few children who treats her just like another kid. As a parent, it is my greatest wish come true." Other parents of children with disabilities have also commented on the impact that inclusion in their school community has had on their child and their family: "There used to be some places that we couldn't go to like a certain house or school or a photography studio because Carla, my daughter with severe disabilities, couldn't do certain things that normal people expect. But now that they know what full inclusion is and how people should help each other, we can go where we want to in comfort" (Grenot-Scheyer, Staub, Schwartz & Peck, 1996).

Benefits and Benevolence

After their sixth-grade year together, Aaron and Cole moved
on to different junior high schools and Cole moved out of his
family house to a group home thirty miles away from Aaron.
Just before their separation, Aaron invited Cole over to his
house to play one Saturday morning. His mother recalled how
it came about:

> Aaron asked me, "Can I have Cole over?" and it really
> stopped me because I kind of thought, *Cole?* And I said,
> "Well, what will you do?" Aaron said, "We'll read books
> and all kinds of things." After that morning I asked
> Aaron, "Why did you invite Cole over?" And I have to
> say I was surprised at his answer. I said, "Is it because
> you wanted to give him the opportunity to be at
> someone's house?" But Aaron said, "No. He's a friend. I
> just want some more time with him before he moves."
> That really blew me away because that is really how he
> perceives Cole—as a friend. The boys spent a wonderful
> morning playing Aaron's guitar, shooting hoops in the
> backyard, and doing Karoke.

A couple of years later I interviewed Aaron about his
friendship with Cole and what he felt about their relationship.
He first informed me that he had recently volunteered to work
that summer at a community center that serves young adults
with disabilities. He was very excited about the opportunity to
work there and he had great hopes that Cole would be in attendance: "I saw Cole's mother the other day at the grocery
store and when she found out that I was working at Hillside
[the community center] she said that she would try really hard
to make sure that Cole could come for at least part of the time.
Maybe the people at his group home could bring him." I asked
Aaron what he felt was the most important thing about his
relationship with Cole. His response was touching: "Knowing

that Cole was comfortable and that he wasn't stressed out. I worked with Cole so he could understand things. I was probably one of the first kids to invite him over to a house. I don't think he ever had been to a friend's house before." Last I asked Aaron whether he felt his relationship with Cole changed his own life or made him a different person. He responded, "Well, knowing Cole has given me a chance to learn how to work and be with people like him, you know, people with disabilities. To work with them. I always thought I might be an architect. But now maybe I will do a job that helps people."

The quality of anyone's life is enhanced by opportunities to develop and maintain friendships with peers and to share the mutual rewards that are possible. When children with disabilities have repeated opportunities to interact with typically developing peers, research has shown improvements in communication skills, social skills, functional skills, and even improved chances to live a more full and normalized life as an adult. Typically developing children and teenagers who tutor or help children with disabilities have better attitudes toward individual human differences, show greater patience and tolerance for other people, feel better about themselves, and are more likely to engage in a relationship with a person with disabilities in their adult lives. Children's friendships with each other may lead to many positive outcomes: companionship, growth in social understanding, increased positive sense of self, development of personal principles, and a sense of belonging. These benefits can occur not only in friendships between typically developing children, but also in friendships between children with and without disabilities such as Aaron and Cole.

In 1989, Robert Bogdan and Steven Taylor presented a paper that sought to understand the perspectives of nondisabled people who do not stigmatize, stereotype, or reject others with obvious disabilities. They argued in their paper that the definition of a person is "found in the relationship between the definer and the defined, not determined either by personal characteristics or the abstract meanings attached to the group of which the person is a part" (p. 136).

These authors described an accepting relationship as one that is long-standing and characterized by closeness and affection and one where the "humanness" of the person with the disability is maintained.

Aaron, Stacy, Theresa, and other typically developing children in this book and elsewhere have "accepting" relationships with peers with disabilities; in essence, they have discovered the "humanness" of their friend. The intent of this chapter was to reveal and highlight the reciprocal benefits that these unique friendships have shared. In the next chapter, the issue of altruism and the characteristics of people who are able to transcend stigmatization or rejection of people with disabilities will be addressed.

References

Anderson, J. & Farron-Davis, F. (1987). A longitudinal comparison of parental expectations for their severely disabled sons and daughters attending integrated and segregated programs. San Francisco, CA: California Research Institute.

Bigelow, B.J. (1977). Children's friendship expectations: A cognitive-developmental study. *Child Development, 48,* 246-253.

Bigelow, B.J. & La Gaipa, J.J. (1975). Children's written descriptions of friendship: A multidimensional analysis. *Developmental Psychology, 11,*105-116.

Biklen, D., Corrigan, C., & Quick, D. (1989). Beyond obligation: Students' relations with each other in integrated classes. In D. Lipsky & A. Gartner (Eds.), *Beyond separate education: Quality education for all* (pp. 207-221). Baltimore, MD: Paul H. Brookes.

Berndt, T.J. (1982). The features and effects of friendship in early adolescence. *Child Development, 53,* 1447-1460.

Billingsley, F., Gallucci, C., Peck, C.A., Schwartz, I.S., & Staub, D. (1996). "But those kids can't even do math: An alternative conceptualization of outcomes for inclusive education."

Bogdan, R. & Taylor, S.J. (1989). Relationships with severely disabled people: The social construction of humanness. *Social Problems, 36,* (2), 135-148.

Doyle, A., Connolly, J., & Rivest, L. (1980). The effects of playmate familiarity on the social interactions of young children. *Child Development, 51,* 217-223.

Goldstein, H. & Wickstrom, S. (1986). Peer intervention effects on communicative interaction among handicapped and nonhandicapped preschoolers. *Journal of Applied Behavior Analysis, 19,* 209-214.

Grenot-Scheyer, M., Staub, D., Peck, C.A., & Schwartz, I.S. (in press). Reciprocity in friendships: Listening to the voices of children and youth with and without disabilities. In L. Meyer, M. Grenot-Scheyer, B. Harry, H. Park, & I. Schwartz (Eds.), *Understanding the social lives of children and youth*. Baltimore, MD: Paul H. Brookes.

Guralnick, M.J. (1990c). Social competence and early intervention. *Journal of Early Intervention, 14,* (1), 3-14.

Halvorsen, A.T. & Sailor, W. (1990). Integration of students with severe and profound disabilities: A review of research. In R. Gaylord-Ross (Ed.), *Issues and research in special education (Vol. 1).* New York: Teachers College Press (pp. 110-172).

Helmstetter, E., Peck, C.A., & Giangreco, M.F. (1994). Outcomes of interactions with peers with moderate or severe disabilities: A statewide survey of high school students. *Journal of the Association for Persons with Severe Handicaps, 19,* (4), 263-276.

Hill, B., Lakin, C., & Bruininks, R. (1984). Trends in residential services for people who are mentally retarded: 1977-1982. *Journal of the Association for Persons with Severe Handicaps, 9,* (4), 243-250.

Hunt, P., Alwell, M., & Goetz, L. (1988). Acquisition of conversation skills and the reduction of inappropriate social interaction behaviors. *Journal of the Association for Persons with Severe Handicaps, 13,* (1), 20-27.

Kishi, G.S. & Meyer, L.H. (1994). What children report and remember: A six-year follow-up of the effects of social contact between peers with and without severe disabilities. *Journal of the Association for Persons with Severe Handicaps, 19,* (4), 277-289.

Lord, C. & Hopkins, J. (1986). The social behavior of autistic children with younger and same-age nonhandicapped peers. *Journal of Autism and Developmental Disorders, 16,* (3), 249-262.

Mannarino, A.P. (1980). The development of children's friendships. In H.C. Foot, A.J. Chapman, and J.R. Smith, (Eds.), *Friendship and Social Relations in Children.* New York: John Wiley & Sons Ltd.

Murata, C. (1984). The effects of an indirect training procedure for nonhandicapped peers on interaction response class behaviors of autistic children. In R. Gaylord-Ross, T. Haring, C. Breen, M. Lee, V. Pitts-Conway, & B. Rogers (Eds.), *The social development of handicapped students.* San Francisco, CA: San Francisco State University.

Murray-Seegert, C. (1989). *Nasty girls, thugs, and humans like us: Social relations between severely disabled and nondisabled students in high school.* Baltimore, MD: Paul H. Brookes.

Park, H. & Goetz, L. (1985). Differences between students with severe disabilities in differing educational programs. Unpublished manuscript. San Francisco, CA: San Francisco State University.

Peck, C.A., Carlson, P., & Helmstetter, E. (1992). Parent and teacher perceptions of outcomes for typically developing children enrolled in integrated early childhood programs: A statewide survey. *Journal of Early Intervention, 16,* 53-63.

Peck, C.A., Donaldson, J., & Pezzoli, M. (1990). Some benefits nonhandicapped adolescents perceive for themselves from their social relationships with peers who have severe handicaps. *Journal of the Association for Persons with Severe Handicaps, 15,* (4), 241-249.

Pumpian, I., Shepard, H., & West, E. (1986). Negotiating job training stations with employers. In P. Wehman & M. Sherrill Moon (Eds.), *Vocational education for persons with handicaps* (pp. 177-192). Baltimore, MD: Paul H. Brookes.

Sapon-Shevin, M. (1990). Initial steps for developing a caring school. In W. Stainback & S. Stainback (Eds.), *Support networks for inclusive schooling* (pp. 241-248). Baltimore, MD: Paul H. Brookes.

Schactili, L. (1987). The effects of trained and untrained peer tutors on social behavior of severely disabled students. Unpublished master's thesis, California State University, Hayward, Department of Special Education, California Research Institute.

Selby, P. (1984). A comparison of learning acquisition by teacher instruction and handicapped peer tutor instruction on leisure and gross motor skills of three mentally retarded children. Unpublished master's thesis, San Francisco State University, San Francisco, CA.

Staub, D. (1995). Perceived outcomes of inclusive education: What do parents of typically developing children think. Unpublished manuscript. Seattle, WA: Inclusive Education Research Group.

Staub, D., Spaulding, M., Peck, C.A., Gallucci, C., & Schwartz, I. (1996). Using nondisabled peers to support the inclusion of students with disabilities at the junior high school level. *Journal of the Association for Persons with Severe Handicaps 21* (4), 194-205.

Staub, D., Schwartz, I.S., Gallucci, C., & Peck, C.A. (1994). Four portraits of friendship at an inclusive school. *Journal of the Association for Persons with Severe Handicaps, 19,* 290-301.

Voeltz, L.M. (1980). Children's attitudes toward handicapped peers. *American Journal of Mental Deficiency, 84,* (3), 455-464.

Voeltz, L.M. (1982). Effects of structured interactions with severely handicapped peers on children's attitudes. *American Journal of Mental Deficiency, 86* (4), 380-390.

Voeltz, L.M. & Brennan, J. (1983). Analysis of the interactions between nonhandicapped and severely handicapped peers using multiple measures. In J.M. Berg (Ed.), *Perspectives and progress in mental retardation, Chapter VI: Social psychology and educational aspects.* Baltimore, MD: University Park Press.

Chapter 6

Acceptance, Altruism, and Advocacy

"Kindness can become its own motive. We are made kind by being kind." (Eric Hoffer)

On this cold, wet November day, the majority of fourth-, fifth-, and sixth- grade students at Jane Austen Elementary have elected to stay indoors for their morning recess. Even though these children are well acclimated to the soggy, gray days of early Winter in the Northwest, today looks even more discouraging than usual. The fields are muddy, the "Big Toy" is wet, and the drizzle hasn't let up for hours. Brittany is one of the few who has decided to brave the conditions. Today is her day to be Ray's "buddy." She has waited almost two weeks for her turn to come around again and she wants to take advantage of it. She knows how much Ray enjoys the Big Toy and she plans to ensure that he has a chance to play on it. She carefully bundles him up, zipping his coat to his chin, and placing his hat on his head, all the while speaking quietly but excitedly to him: "We're going outside, Ray. I'm going to take you to the Big Toy." Ray appears to be listening to Brittany as he slows down his rocking and tilts his head toward her. Once he is dressed warmly, Brittany squeals, "Let's go, Ray!" She opens the back door, grabs Ray by the hand, and heads him outside. Ray's teaching assistant sees their exit from across the room and hurries to grab her own coat and follow them. She yells to Brittany, "You forgot your coat. It's too cold to be out today without one." Brittany turns back, smiles at the teaching assistant, and replies, "I'm okay. I don't even feel cold."

Ray and Brittany walk side by side to the Big Toy structure. Ray has his hand on Brittany's back. They do not make eye contact but Brittany talks to him the whole way: "Look Ray, it's still raining. Can you believe it? Look at the big puddle. It has a rainbow in it. I wonder if all the worms are coming out on the grass because of the rain. Boy, I bet the birds love these days!" When they arrive at the Big Toy, Ray goes directly to the slide. The teaching assistant, Ms. Jones, has caught up to the children and quickly pulls out a communication card with a picture of a slide on it. She asks Ray, "Do you want the slide?" Ray grabs at the card and then drops it to the ground. He walks to the ladder and begins his climb up. He has made his choice. Ms. Jones stands behind him and Brittany waits at the base of the slide. When Ray gets to the top, she smiles and says, "Come down the slide, Ray." Ray lets go of the edges of the slide until he reaches the bottom. Brittany tells him, "That was fun." Ray gives her a rare smile and takes her hand to lead her around the structure to do it again. For a brief moment, they make eye contact. Then Ray climbs to the top and Brittany goes back to the bottom to catch him.

A *Social Construction* of "*Humanness*"

Even though Ray is nonverbal, seldom expresses pleasure, will pointedly ignore people talking to him, drools, has seizures, engages in stereotypical rocking behavior, and frequently has loud shrieking outbursts, Brittany accepts Ray for who he is. She respects him as a human being who has feelings, rights, and opinions.

In their study on typically developing people who do not stigmatize, stereotype, or reject those with obvious disabilities such as Ray's, Robert Bogdan and Steven Taylor (1989) identified four dimensions that are associated with defining another as human. The first is attributing thinking to the other. These authors found that the nondisabled people in their study believed and cited evidence that their partners with severe disabilities can and do think. Certainly Brittany believes that Ray "thinks" and has an opinion. She knows that Ray likes the Big Toy and wants to go there during recess time. How does Brittany know what Ray is "thinking?" One possibility is that she puts herself in Ray's position or "takes the role of Ray." She becomes empathetic to his feelings. When I asked Brittany how she knows what Ray wants, she explained, "Like my shirt sleeve. He tugs on it and I just follow him because I know he wants to show me something real interesting."

The second dimension that the nondisabled people in Bogdan and Taylor's study used in "constructing" their companions with severe disabilities as persons was to see them as individuals. They were able to identify the unique personalities, likes and dislikes, life histories, and appearances that their friends and loved ones with severe disabilities had. Brittany is very aware of Ray's unique qualities. Furthermore, she views these qualities as individual to Ray, not specific to his disability. For example, Brittany knows that Ray likes reading books while sitting on the couch. She also knows that he doesn't like hard-textured food, as this brief excerpt reveals:

> It was snack time for Ray. Brittany asked Ray if he was
> going to eat his cookie. She told the teaching assistant
> that he didn't like the texture of hard foods and sug-
> gested dipping the cookie in water; "That's what he
> does all the time to soften his cookie," Brittany said.
> The teaching assistant dipped the cookie and handed it
> to Ray, who took a big bite.

Brittany understands that like everyone else Ray has his "good" days and his "bad" days. She is sensitive to his feelings, and when he isn't feeling well, she makes sure she gives him the space he needs. Brittany has called Ray at home and knows from talking to his mother that Ray has a big back yard with horses and several dogs. She uses this knowledge at school to communicate with Ray and engage him in social interactions:

> It was choice time in the classroom. Ray and Brittany
> were sitting together at the reading area and Brittany
> was trying to get Ray to look at some pictures. She
> picked up one book and showed Ray the cover, which
> had a picture of a horse on it. She said to him, "Look
> Ray. Here is a horse. You have a horse at home.' Ray
> leaned over and looked at the picture briefly. He
> seemed to be listening to Brittany.

Viewing the other as reciprocating was the third dimension that Bogdan and Taylor found among the nondisabled people they interviewed. The nondisabled people in their study saw the person with disabilities as giving back something important to the relationship. They mentioned deriving pleasure from their relationships because they liked their companion with disabilities and enjoyed spending time with them. For some, the person with disabilities was an important source of companionship. Several mentioned how the people with disabilities had expanded their own lives by helping them meet new people and learn about aspects of their communities that they had not known about previously. Finally, some identified a sense of accomplishment in contributing to the well-being and personal growth of their friend with a disability. They saw positive changes occurring in their friends. All of these benefits were highlighted in the previous chapter, and they were just as apparent for Ray and Brittany. These two children enjoyed the companionship that the other offered. Brittany felt good about "helping" Ray, and Ray benefited from his relationship with Brittany because she took the time to understand him.

The fourth and final dimension that Bogdan and Taylor found in their study was that the nondisabled participants defined their partners with disabilities as full and important members of their social units; consequently, they created a social place for them. They also defined a role for the people with disabilities in the rituals and routines of the social community. Brittany, as well as many other classmates and Ray's teachers, viewed Ray as an important member of their classroom and school community. Likewise, Brittany's unique relationship with Ray gave her an opportunity to further define her role as a member of their fourth- and fifth-grade classrooms. This was a nice benefit for Brittany since she was a new student to the school during her fourth-grade year. Her relationship with Ray gave her a starting point for belonging. The importance of membership for the development of social relationships, and vice versa, was also seen as an important reciprocal outcome of children's friendships. Ray's and Brittany's friendship was no exception.

Bogdan and Taylor concluded their paper by addressing the ethical issues and debates surrounding the treatment of infants, children, and adults with severe disabilities. They wrote: "Whether or not people with severe disabilities will be treated as human beings or persons is not a matter of their physical or mental condition. It is a matter of definition. We can show that they, and we, are human by including, by accepting them rather than separating them out" (p. 140). The previous chapter in this book, as well as other research in the area, has shown that one possible outcome of relationships between children and adolescents with and without disabilities is the development of personal principles that may lead to greater commitment to moral and ethical concerns. What moral behaviors can we expect from children? Can children be altruistic, and how do their friendships with each other affect their prosocial behaviors such as helping, sharing, and comforting? How can adults facilitate and support children's moral growth? Although an entire book could be devoted to addressing these questions, the remainder of this chapter will attempt to provide at least some basic answers.

Morality, Altruism, and Prosocial Behavior

According to William Damon (1988), an expert in the field of child development and ethics, morality arises naturally out of people's social relationships with others and children's morality is no exception. However, Damon warns that moral reactions in children are easy to overlook if we expect them to be expressed in ways that are similar to an adult's. He has found that children experience many moral feelings in their social interactions with others. As children reflect on their moral feelings, they question and redefine the values that gave rise to the feelings. Sooner or later, the redefined values are tested through their behaviors, all of which bring up new feelings, new reflections, and further redefinitions of the child's moral code. In short, children's sense of morality is constantly being shaped and reshaped by their experiences.

EMPATHY: A BUILDING BLOCK FOR ALTRUISM

Empathy is one of the "core" emotions that most social scientists believe is necessary for the development of morality and other prosocial behaviors. Empathy means reacting to another's feelings with an emotional response that is similar to the other's. In an empathetic response, one becomes pleased by another's joy and upset by another's pain. Although empathy is experienced as an emotional state, it has a cognitive as well as an emotional component. In order to understand another's feelings, a child must first recognize the other's feelings. This cognitive ability to determine another's inner psychological states is called perspective taking. Brittany and many of the other children described in this book were able to take the perspective of their friends with disabilities and react empathetically toward them. In some situations this was a tricky skill. For example, Ray did not talk, so Brittany had to find alternative ways to interpret Ray's feelings. Brittany told me about an incident that illustrated how she could be empathetic to Ray during an upsetting time:

> It was after school and I was walking to day care and there was a new lady with Ray and another boy from the class who didn't even know what Ray's bus number was. The number had changed. And Ray was very upset. He kept trying to turn around and go the other way and he was whining and fussing and crying. He was all upset because the bus wasn't where it usually was and the new lady didn't understand that. I told Ray, 'Don't worry, it should be there.' I'm his friend so I knew why he was upset.

Children's moral reasoning goes through a sequence of changes from their late preschool years into adolescence. Preschool children use more self-indulgent and needs-oriented reasoning. Although they will show concern for other children in distress, their actions are likely to be determined by their own needs and comfort level. For example, they may share a favorite toy with a child who is upset if they know they will get the toy back or aren't that interested in the toy at that moment. In elementary school, children's actions begin to reflect their concern with others' opinions and approval of them. At this stage, most children have stereotypic conceptions of "good" and "bad" behavior. They may not be able to explain why they are being helpful, but they know it is "the right thing to do." In contrast, high school-aged students can verbalize self-reflective empathy. They know *why* it is "the right thing to do." Older children are more capable of understanding others' perspectives, as well as the ways in which others may view their behaviors.

In late childhood, ages 10 to 12, children also further develop their capacity for empathy. At this stage, children begin to show empathy for people who live in generally unfortunate circumstances. Their concern is no longer limited to the feelings of particular persons in situations that the child is directly involved with (Damon, 1988).

SHARING AND PROSOCIAL BEHAVIORS

There is no better evidence of a child's sense of fairness than the act of sharing. Sharing is one of the rituals of childhood that young children naturally discover and enjoy. Most children delight in the balance and predictability of turn-taking that comes from sharing. Empathy provides a compelling motive for altruistic acts like sharing. A child witnessing another child in distress sometimes will experience the other's sorrow and react by offering a toy to comfort him. Empathy provides children with their first instinctive moral sense of obligation to share. It is around age four that the combination of natural empathetic awareness and adult encouragement leads a child to develop a firm sense of the need to share with others (Damon, 1988).

By the beginning of elementary school, children begin to express more awareness of the need to be fair to others. They begin to understand the principles of fairness, including equality, merit, and benevolence. Equality means making sure that everyone is treated the same. Merit means giving extra rewards for hard work, for a talented performance, or for some positive activity. Benevolence is giving special consideration for those who are at a disadvantage.

While adults can foster sharing among children, it is the give-and-take of peer requests, arguments, conflicts, and acts of generosity that provide the most immediate motive. The day-to-day construction of fairness standards in social life must be done by children in collaboration with one another (Damon,

1988). Studies have shown that children show a greater tendency to share and cooperate with one another as their moral understanding develops. With age and developing moral values, they become increasingly generous and helpful in their everyday behavior. Sharing becomes a dominant characteristic of relationships with other children, rather than just an occasional act. Furthermore, children's understanding of fairness becomes more sophisticated as their ideas about equality, merit, benevolence, and compromise are established.

Many of the typically developing children who have been described in this book showed a deep sense of fairness toward their companions with disabilities. Brittany felt very strongly that Ray should be treated equally and respectfully. Her mother shared with me that Brittany would come home upset about Ray's toileting accidents at school. She said that Brittany didn't want Ray to feel embarrassed or ashamed of the accidents. She thought the reason that Brittany empathized so much about Ray's accidents was that her younger sister had bladder control problems for which she took medication. Brittany understood how traumatized her sister was when she had an accident at school and she didn't want Ray to experience the same feelings or possible ridicule from his peers.

In addition to having empathy for Ray, Brittany also interacted with Ray in a manner that was considered prosocial. Prosocial actions, such as helping, sharing, and comforting others, often include some cost, self-sacrifice, or risk on the part of the actor. Prosocial behavior is distinguished from moral judgment, a term that refers to the cognitive aspects of morality, including conceptualizations and reasoning about moral issues. Prosocial behavior also differs from altruism, which is generally defined as regard for or devotion to the interests of others. Altruistic acts involve some degree of conscious decision-making. Because altruistic behavior is by definition intentional and voluntary, it must be preceded by some thought to the behavior to be performed (Mussen & Eisenberg-Berg, 1977). In contrast, prosocial behaviors are often unconscious.

The acts of caring, sharing, and helping are shaped by many factors, including age, personality characteristics, motivations, capabilities, judgments, ideas, and the immediate contexts encountered. Interestingly, one factor that does not seem to affect prosocial behavior is gender. Despite the stereotype that girls share, help, and comfort other people more than boys do, most studies have found no gender differences in children's prosocial behaviors (Eisenberg, 1992). Strong predispositions to prosocial behavior in preschool and elementary-aged children are often associated with having high ego strength, self-control, and good personal adjustment. Children who are sympathetic seem to be especially likely to engage in prosocial actions.

Although prosocial behavior often seems to come more naturally to some children than to others, that does not mean that it cannot be learned. In fact, it is through friendships that many children learn and polish their understandings of moral behavior. Since this has been an area of considerable research over the centuries, the next section examines the connection between friendship and prosocial behavior in detail.

Friendship and Morality

At its best, friendship can create an ideal moral condition. In true friendship, the welfare of each party is seen as equally important. There is respect for the other's rights and concern for the other's well-being. It may well be that friendship is the primary context in which children acquire certain key behavioral norms and moral standards. (Damon, 1988).

Jean Piaget, well known for his study of child development, described children's social interactions, especially during the middle years of childhood, as essential to the development of mature moral thought (1965). During middle childhood, he hypothesized that there was a decline in children's egocentrism, an increase in their role-taking skills, and heightened sensitivity to the experiences of others. A primary cause for these changes was thought to be the increased reciprocity and egalitarianism that becomes evident in children's friendships.

Children's interactions provide many natural opportunities for acts of altruism. For example, sharing play materials and collaborating or cooperating in the context of fantasy play, games, and task assignments are all typical friendly interactions among peers. Furthermore, experiences with friends can affect future prosocial acts with nonfriends in two ways. First, as the result of interactions with a specific friend, children may change their view of all social relationships. After sharing a friend's joys and sorrows, they may empathize more with people they do not know well. Second, after using certain principles of fairness with friends, children may begin to regard these principles as generally applicable (Rubin & Ross, 1982).

Moral living revolves around the assumption that social actions are reciprocal. Reciprocity in social relationships is defined most simply as a principle of give-and-take. Of all the social norms, reciprocity is the only one considered necessary for the very existence of relationships (Mannarino, 1980). Once relationships are established, reciprocity maintains them by ensuring that exchanges between partners serve the interests of both people. This balance of interest in the relationship prevents it from breaking down. Children's friendships also promote feelings of mutuality and intimacy. Mutuality means a high level of joint participation in collaborative activities. Intimacy means a close, affectionate bond leading to the shared disclosure of secrets and other confidences. Because of their interpersonal value, mutuality and intimacy contribute indirectly but importantly to children's moral awareness and learning (Damon, 1988).

William Bukowski and Lorrie Sippola argue that friendship and morality are interrelated (1996). They propose that friendship is defined by moral parameters and serves as a context in which morality is learned and achieved. These authors have identified five themes in Aristotle's model of friendship and morality to guide their ideas of how the two are related. Aristotle's themes are:

1. Goodness is characteristic of the highest form of friendship;
2. Goodness is required if a person is to appreciate friendship;
3. The goal of the highest form of friendship is rooted in goodness;
4. Friendship is a relationship between equals;
5. Friendship requires both justice and benevolence.

Furthermore, Bukowski and Sippola found that Aristotle distinguished between three types of friendship:
1. Utility friendship, which is centered on the benefits that one would enjoy as a result of being someone's friend;
2. Pleasure friendship, which is based on one's satisfaction in interacting with another;
3. Goodness friendship, which requires a greater appreciation or understanding of another and is based on the recognition of goodness in the other person.

The first two forms of friendship are essentially self-centered, whereas the third is characterized by virtue, kindness, benevolence, and justice. Aristotle believed that a goal of the highest form of friendship is to do good for one's friend. Furthermore, he proposed that goodness is not just a simple feature of friendship, but the force that holds a friendship together. As a consequence of love between friends, the friends have certain obligations to treat each other in a fair and benevolent manner.

Aristotle's ideas on the link between friendship and morality continue to be represented in the views of many philosophers today. They describe "morally superior friendships" as: "having the qualities of concern, caring, sympathy, sensitivity to a friend's needs or wants, identification with the other and a willingness to give of one's self to a friend" (Bukowski & Sippola, 1996, p. 244). Four particular qualities that are essential for "morally" excellent friendships have been identified:

1. A deep concern for the other for his or her own sake;
2. Intimate knowledge of the emotional and moral world of the other based on mutual self-disclosure;
3. High levels of trust and commitment to the relationship;
4. Conflict resolution styles that contribute to the emotional well-being of the individuals involved (Blum, 1980; Friedman, 1989; Noddings, 1988; Raymond, 1986).

Research has demonstrated that friendship is built upon particular moral principles. Theory proposes that friendship is an important context for the development and emergence of morality. In their relationships with friends, children have opportunities to learn about others' needs and feelings and to experience the desire or motivation to be responsive to these needs. Certainly many of the friendships that are shared in this book illustrate children's growth in their ability to be more responsive and empathetic to their friends' needs.

Promoting Altruism in Children

A significant part of moral development comes through dialogue, reflecting on experience, and looking at how our behavior affects others. Evelyn Schneider, who writes on giving students a voice in the classroom, suggests: "if we want to nurture children who will grow into lifelong learners, into self-directed seekers, into the kind of adults who are morally responsible even when someone is not looking, then we need to give them opportunities to practice making choices and reflecting on the outcomes" (1996, p. 26).

Children's and adults' helping, sharing, and comforting behaviors are all affected by their situation. Recent research also suggests that the reasons individuals give for such prosocial actions can encourage additional prosocial behavior. For example, when adults tell children that their prior positive behaviors were due to internal causes (e.g., kindness), they are more likely to behave in a prosocial manner on subsequent occasions (Eisenberg, 1986).

William Damon (1988) has identified six factors to bear in mind when developing a comprehensive understanding of children's moral education (pp. 117-118):

1. Simply by the virtue of their participation in essential social relationships, children encounter the classic moral issues facing humans everywhere: issues of fairness, honesty, responsibility, kindness, and obedience. Moral awareness comes from within a child's normal social experience.

2. The child's moral awareness is shaped and supported by natural emotional reactions to observations and events.

3. Relations with parents, teachers, and other adults introduce the child to important social standards, rules, and conventions.

4. Relations with peers introduce children to norms of direct reciprocity and to standards of sharing, cooperation, and fairness.

5. Because children's morality is shaped through social influence, broad variations in social experience can lead to broad differences in children's moral orientations.

6. Moral growth in school settings is governed by the same developmental processes that apply to moral growth everywhere.

These considerations reinforce the ideas that children's morality is an outcome of emotional, cognitive, and social forces. Children begin with natural emotional reactions to things that happen in their lives and their reactions are supported, refined, and molded by their relationships with their peers and significant adults. Through participation, observation, and interpretation, children develop their moral ideals.

Based on the above considerations and what we know about a child's moral development, Damon (1988) recommends three measures to implement in schools to promote moral education:

1. Help children reason independently about moral problems;
2. Encourage children's participation in the value of dialogue if moral values are to stick. Little can be gained through one-way exposition and lecturing; and
3. Provide moral mentors for children in schools.

These recommendations, as well as others, will be addressed further in Chapters 9 and 10.

Advocacy, Altruism, and Disability

The above discussion has hopefully helped to clarify the relationship between children's prosocial or moral development and their friendships with peers. Most experts in the field would agree: friendships promote positive moral development in children. On the flip side, a child who typically engages in prosocial behaviors such as sharing, helping, kindness, fairness, and so on is likely to have more satisfactory and positive relationships with his or her peers. Two questions remain. First, do opportunities to socially interact with and befriend children with disabilities enhance and promote the moral development and prosocial behaviors of typically developing children? Second, are typically developing children who are highly moral (i.e., engage in many prosocial behaviors) more likely to befriend and socially interact with children with moderate to severe disabilities? Brittany's friendship with Ray reflects the latter of these two hypotheses.

Brittany first met Ray when she entered fourth grade. Her parents had transferred her to Jane Austen that year because they weren't satisfied with her previous school: "Brittany was attending very traditional based classrooms. Because she is a lateral thinker, the classes there really weren't appropriate for Brittany and she did not grow or blossom. Since she's been here [Jane Austen] she has blossomed and learned how to read" (Brittany's mother). Brittany's mother describes her as a child who lacks any kind of "competitive spirit." She explains, "It's not that Brittany wants to avoid conflict, it's just that things kind of go over her and she doesn't worry about it. She will not get her homework done or other things done because she won't fight for the computer. She feels it's more important for her peers to get access to the computer than for her to."

Brittany's teachers describe her as a "free spirit" and nonconformist who doesn't worry about what other people think of her. When she interacts with Ray, she is unbothered by his screaming or unusual stereotypic behaviors. She chalks it up to the fact that that is who Ray is, a child who occasionally screams out and rocks. When asked to describe Brittany's relationship with Ray, her mother said, "Brittany is a helper to Ray and yet at the same point she looks at helping Ray as being a privilege. She'll come home from school and talk a lot about the things that she did for Ray." When I asked Brittany why she helps Ray, she answered, "Because I like to. It's fun and he really seems to enjoy me helping him." Then I asked her why she thinks Ray needs her help. "Well, because he can't do some things that we can. He can walk, but he can't talk. He has to communicate another way. He doesn't do sign language either. So we need to figure out what he is trying to tell us." While Brittany likes to help Ray, she perceives her relationship with him as even deeper. She once mentioned that she wished Ray was her brother. When asked why, she responded, "Well, because he's different from all the rest of them. It's kind of fun to be with people who are different from you, and I think that if Ray could talk he would want me as his sister too."

Brittany is an example of a child who is kind, fair, and good to the people around her. She could be characterized as having highly developed moral principles for her age. It is likely that because this is the type of child she is, she befriended Ray, a child in need of help, and, in her perception, a friend.

Brittany's mother feels that Brittany also benefits from her friendship with Ray: "Brittany gets the opportunity to see Ray as a person, to get to know that not all people are the same, that they have different abilities and differences. Brittany, unique as she is, benefits from it that way. Also, she needs to be needed. Ray fulfills that need."

Ray also derives benefits from his friendship with Brittany. Perhaps most importantly, Ray has a devoted and passionate advocate in Brittany. Because of her sense of fairness and equality, Brittany strongly believes in, and verbalizes the importance of Ray's membership in his general education classrooms. She questions and challenges Ray's removal from their classroom. Their fourth-grade teacher shared an example:

> Brittany definitely keeps us on our toes. One day last week Ray was really having a hard time—lots of screaming and fussing. I asked his teaching assistant to take him for a walk. I was stressed that the kids were getting stressed. Brittany came up to me and said, "I think we should ignore Ray's screaming and find something that he wants to do in class. Think how bad he feels being sent out of the room." Well, how do you respond to that? What it did was really force me to push for a better communication system on his part and the special education staff have really responded positively.

In Brittany's case Ray has provided her with a way to express all the prosocial behaviors that she seems to be bursting with. Her teachers and mother agree—Brittany is a unique child in that regard.

For many of the typically developing children described in this book, as well as elsewhere, their friendships with peers with disabilities have provided them with opportunities to express and practice prosocial behaviors. Perhaps it is because their peers with disabilities offer a safe way for them to show kind and caring interactions. For example, Aaron was not self-conscious about his affectionate and loving interactions with Cole, which seems surprising for a sixth-grade boy. So often the peer pressures to "be cool" at this age interfere with children's expressions of compassion to one another. But no one ridiculed Aaron for his behavior toward Cole. In fact, Aaron was admired by his peers because of his relationship with Cole. Like Brittany, Aaron became an advocate for his friend with a disability. When the sixth graders got ready for their annual overnight camping trip, Aaron was the first to make sure that Cole would be able to attend.

In a context that promotes cooperation and caring among peers, the inclusion of children with moderate and severe disabilities may very well be the ideal stimulus for supporting the development of prosocial and altruistic behavior among typically developing children. Furthermore, as children experience moral growth in areas of fairness and equality, their motivation to advocate for their peers with disabilities may be enhanced. While these beliefs have never been systematically addressed by research, Brittany's and Ray's story, as well as many others, reveal further evidence of the potential reciprocal benefits of friendship between children with and without disabilities.

References

Bogdan, R. & Taylor, S.J. (1989). Relationships with severely disabled people: The social construction of humanness. *Social Problems, 36,* (2), 135-148.

Blum, L. (1980). *Friendship, altruism, and morality.* London: Routledge and Kegan Paul.

Bukowski, W.M. & Sippola, L.K. (1996). Friendship and morality: (How) are they related? In W.M. Bukowski, A.F. Newcomb, & W.W. Hartup (Eds.), *The company they keep: Friendship in childhood and adolescence.* New York, NY: Cambridge University Press.

Damon, W. (1988). *The moral child: Nurturing children's natural moral growth.* New York: Free Press.

Eisenberg, N. (1986). *Altruistic emotion, cognition, and behavior.* Hillsdale, NJ: Erlbaum.

Eisenberg, N. (1992). *The caring child.* Cambridge, MA: Harvard University Press.

Friedman, M. (1989). Friendship and moral growth. *The Journal of Value Inquiry, 23,* 3-13.

Mannarino, A.P. (1980). The development of children's friendships. In H.C. Foot, A.J. Chapman, and J.R. Smith (Eds.), *Friendship and social relations in children.* John Wiley & Sons Ltd.

Mussen, P. & Eisenberg-Berg, N. (1977). Roots of caring, sharing, and helping: The development of prosocial behavior in children. San Francisco: W.H. Freeman and Company.

Noddings, N. (1984). *Caring: A feminine approach to ethics and moral education.* Berkeley: University of California.

Piaget, J. (1965). *The moral judgment of the child.* New York: The Free Press.

Raymond, J. (1986). *A passion for friends.* Boston: Beacon.

Schneider, E. (1996). Giving students a voice in the classroom. *Educational Leadership,* 22-26.

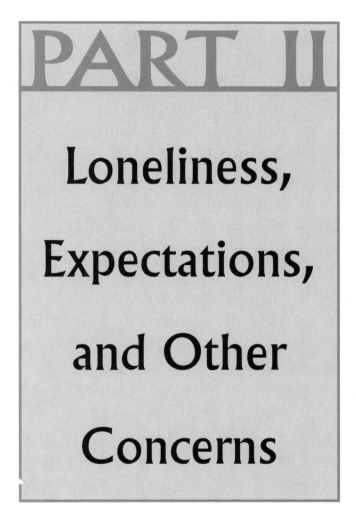

PART II

Loneliness, Expectations, and Other Concerns

Chapter 7

Loneliness & Disability:
The Dark Side

*"Loneliness and the feeling of being unwanted is the most
terrible poverty." (Mother Theresa)*

Mr. Allen's fourth-grade class hurries into the cafeteria for lunch this sunny day in December. It is seldom that they are the first class in the usually busy, crowded room. They rejoice in having this large, empty space to themselves by chatting excitedly to each other, slapping "high fives," and being silly. Those who have brought sack lunches seat themselves noisily at their assigned table and begin to eat. Those who are buying lunch make their way through the food line, selecting items from the pizza and salad bars. Lindsey, a 10-year-old with mild learning disabilities, is the last of Mr. Allen's students to enter the cafeteria. Unlike many of her classmates, she does not notice that today they are the first class in the large room, nor do any of her classmates comment to her about this fact. Her long blonde hair falls in her face as she scuffles toward the lunch line. She fills her tray without acknowledging the lunch helpers and takes a seat at the far end of an empty table behind the one where the majority of her classmates sit. She is not invited to join their table, even though room could easily be made.

Several minutes later, Corrie's fifth-sixth, multi-grade class enters the lunch room. By now the cafeteria is bustling with noisy, hungry children. Corrie, an 11-year-old with moderate mental retardation, has brought a sack lunch as usual. Without as much as a glance around, she sits down at the nearest table and begins to open her lunch. She carefully unwraps her peanut butter and jelly sandwich and places it delicately on a pink napkin. Next to that she puts her orange wedges, bag of chips, and cookies. The only emotion to pass over her face is a brief look of disappointment when she counts only three cookies instead of the usual four. Her mother has recently become concerned about Corrie's growing weight and is trying to cut back on the sweets. Since she has entered the cafeteria, Corrie has spoken to no one.

Lindsey continues to eat her lunch alone and is only half finished when the cafeteria starts to empty. The children who have finished lunch are being dismissed for outside recess. Across the room, Lindsey notices Corrie. She gives Corrie a little wave but Corrie is focused on her lunch. Lindsey finishes another bite of pizza, empties her lunch tray, and sits down next to Corrie. Corrie looks up at Lindsey, and, without a word, offers Lindsey one of her treasured cookies. Lindsey smiles, says "thanks" to Corrie, and waits patiently as Corrie finishes her lunch. The girls don't talk but share a companionable silence. When Corrie finally finishes her lunch, Lindsey helps her with her trash. "Let's go Corrie," she says, "we still have time to play outside." Corrie looks at Lindsey and in a loud, articulate voice, says, "Yeah! Let's go!" For the first time that day, both girls are animated and happy. They walk quickly through the cafeteria to the playground. Corrie pushes the door open, and, as a blast of cold December air washes over her, she looks up at the bright sun and yells, "Yippee!" before she runs off to the open playing field. Lindsey laughs and runs after her.

A Story of Loneliness

Until Corrie and Lindsey became friends in their third-fourth, multi-grade class, neither had experienced a long-lasting, friendly relationship with another child. The hypothesized reasons for their lack of friendships are markedly different. Furthermore, their lack of friends was also perceived very differently by the adults in their lives. For instance, Corrie's mother and teachers described Corrie as asocial, a loner, someone who chooses not to have relationships with other children. When asked to describe Corrie's social personality, her mother had this to say:

> Corrie would be the perfect only child. I've never had to entertain her. And Troy [Corrie's brother] goes nuts if he doesn't have a friend with him at all times. I mean it's like his entire friend group is so crucial. Corrie has learned to entertain herself. She'll spend hours alone.

Lindsey, on the other hand, is described as difficult to get along with, as having poor self-esteem and social skills that inhibit her ability to make friends. When asked to describe Lindsey, her mother explained:

> I would describe Lindsey as a very emotional child, one who gets easily upset over things. She doesn't necessarily do well with kids her own age, but she does better with younger children. Maybe because she is slower in reading and stuff than her classmates. Maybe she feels more comfortable with younger kids. Since we've moved here [Jane Austen Elementary] Lindsey hasn't invited anyone over or anything except for Corrie.

Lindsey's and Corrie's social history reveals two girls who have been friendless for the majority of their lives. They have never slept over at another child's house, they haven't had intimate chats about life with a peer, and their birthday parties, if attended by nonfamily members, were orchestrated by well-meaning parents who designed the guest list and hand picked the guests. At school, their lunch periods, recesses, and free times occur without the company of other children who play with them, talk to them, or share meals with them. Lindsey is quite aware of this gap in her life: "I haven't made any friends yet in my class this year [her fourth grade year]. And now I'm moving again. I know that I didn't have any friends when I first came here—I was a little pain in the rear end. And I don't know anyone where we're moving." Corrie, described as "oblivious to the social milieu around her," was animated, enthusiastic, happy, and talkative in the presence of her friend, Lindsey. Interestingly, the concern that either Corrie or Lindsey were lonely was never expressed by their parents or teachers. Rather, their immediate concerns were related to their "behavioral" issues.

Corrie's "running away" and leaving the school grounds has been a long-standing safety issue for her. Consequently, for much of her school day, she was accompanied by an adult who kept a close watch on her. After Corrie became Lindsey's friend in Corrie's fourth-grade year, she stopped running away. Lindsey's behavioral issues were also long-standing and reflected in the "charts" that moved with her to the many elementary schools she attended. Before even giving themselves a chance to know her, Lindsey's teachers expected a toughened, aggressive, stubborn, and apathetic student who had difficulties in reading and writing. When Lindsey moved to Jane Austen Elementary her third-grade year, she was placed in the same third-fourth, multi-grade class as Corrie. Their teacher, noticing Lindsey's need to practice her reading skills, assigned Lindsey to read to Corrie and another nonreader in their class each day. Corrie and Lindsey connected immediately, perhaps because their common need for a friend was so obvious. Once Lindsey's and Corrie's friendship was established, their behavior issues went away and there was positive growth in their social behaviors.

The importance of friendships for ALL children has been a theme from the beginning of this book and it has been a topic of interest for social scientists, educators, and parents for many years. But what do we know about children without friends? Only in the past ten years have researchers who have studied the issue of loneliness for the adult population begun to focus on the effects and ramifications for lonely children. Furthermore, the research and discussion on loneliness for children with mild disabilities is sparse and almost nonexistent for children with moderate and severe disabilities. What *is* loneliness and why are children lonely? What about children with disabilities who are lacking in social skills as well as equal opportunities to be included with their typically developing peers in social settings? What does loneliness mean for them and what can the significant adults in these children's lives do to address this issue?

Lonely People, Lonely Lives

WHAT IS LONELINESS?

Most of us have felt lonely at least once in our lives. The feeling may have been brief and fleeting or lasted for several months, even years. If asked to describe the feeling, the adjectives uncomfortable, painful, depressing, and miserable probably come to mind. According to Steven Duck (1991), a social scientist, isolation and aloneness are different from loneliness. Loneliness is a feeling about isolation, and people can be isolated without feeling lonely just as they can feel lonely in a crowd. Isolation is physical separation from other people, but loneliness is the feeling that you do not have as many friends, or the sorts of friends, that you wish you had, or enough of the opportunities to meet potential friends as you might desire. Additionally, Duck (1991) discriminates between "state" loneliness, which lasts as long as the provoking circumstances (such as those first days in summer camp when you haven't made a friend yet), and "trait" loneliness, which is the persistent, long-term loneliness that some people experience.

Loneliness is characterized by unpleasant, painful, or anxious feelings that occur as a result of having fewer or less satisfying personal relationships than an individual desires (Ponzetti, 1990). Children, as well as adults, have a natural human need for emotional intimacy in relationships and when disruption occurs in those relationships, loneliness results. Furthermore, it is possible for people to have friendships and family ties and yet still be lonely because their relationships do not provide them with the satisfaction they desire. Studies also suggest that the quality of social interaction is more predictive of loneliness than the quantity of social interaction (Larson, 1990).

Richard Amado (1993), in his chapter on loneliness among adults with developmental disabilities, drew three central conclusions regarding loneliness from the works of experts in the field, Hojat and Crandall (1989), Perlman and Peplau (1982), and Weiss (1982). He concluded that:

1. Loneliness is a subjective event, a feeling that is individually defined (e.g., given the same set of circumstances, one person might experience loneliness and another person might not);
2. The quality of social relationships, not just the quantity of social contacts, affects the feeling of loneliness and associated behaviors;
3. Loneliness is an unpleasant condition, an aversive context in which to live (p. 68).

WHO ARE THE LONELY?

Researchers have estimated that more than 10 percent of children in grades three to six report that they feel lonely and do not have anyone to play with (Asher, Hymel, & Renshaw, 1984; Luftig, 1987). Research findings also indicate that about 5 to 10 percent of elementary school children are named as a friend by no one in their class. Unfortunately, based on loneliness scores collected over one year, the feelings of loneliness among this age group of children remain relatively stable (Hymel, 1994). Consequently, the feelings of loneliness that these children are experiencing are not just fleeting or momentary.

Children without friends are not a homogeneous group. According to Steven Asher and Peter Renshaw (1981), they can be divided into two categories: children who are neglected and children who are rejected. The children who fall in the neglected category receive few, if any, positive or negative nominations as friends from their peer group. To their peers they seem quiet and untalkative. They are invisible. Corrie easily fit into this category. Because she exhibited very limited social skills and competence, Corrie seldom initiated interactions of any kind with her peers. Although she displayed some odd, autistic-like behaviors, they were not loud or noticeable; she did not stand out in a crowd. Her major behavioral concern, her running away behavior, resulted in an adult instructional aide being assigned to stay by her side. The presence of this aide created a further barrier to interactions she might have had with peers. After several years of being "placed" in inclusive settings, Corrie remained isolated, separate, and alone.

The children who fall into the "rejected" category also receive few, if any, positive nominations from their peers. They do, however, receive negative nominations and are described as unpleasant or uncomfortable to be around. The children who are rejected by their peers in school report some of the highest degrees of loneliness (Bullock, 1993). They are rejected for a variety of reasons, ranging from being aggressive with peers, having difficulty communicating their needs and desires, and misinterpreting intentions of other children, to rejecting a peer's suggestion without offering a reason, ignoring others, and being disruptive. Rejected children are also at a greater risk for school adjustment problems and they report lower levels of self-esteem than their nonrejected peers.

Research in the area of learning disabilities has so consistently linked social skills deficits with peer rejection that it has been suggested that such difficulties be considered criteria for defining learning disabilities (Coleman, McHam, & Minnett, 1992). Although Lindsey's status with her peers was not formally evaluated, she often displayed the behaviors described above as typical of rejected children. A brief excerpt from observation notes taken of Lindsey's interactions with a classmate reveals a common scenario for her:

> Carin, the girl next to Lindsey, accidentally bumped her in the arm. Lindsey gave her a look and told her to "knock it off." Carin said to Lindsey, "I didn't do it on purpose" and the two argued back and forth until the teacher looked over and told them to get back to work. They stayed quiet for a couple of minutes and then started up again. One of the special education teachers came in the room to talk with Lindsey and told her she didn't have time to work with her today. Lindsey tried to involve her in the argument with Carin, but the special education teacher just told Lindsey to move to another seat if she didn't want to be by her. Lindsey moved, but flashed Carin "bad looks" every time she could.

It is important to note that using sociometric methodology (in which peers characterize each other's social status) to categorize children as rejected or neglected is not always a predictor of whether a child feels lonely. Not all rejected or neglected children feel lonely, and, on the contrary, some well-accepted children do. While Lindsey readily shared her feelings of loneliness, Corrie seldom appeared lonely or expressed feelings of loneliness to the people around her. The fact remains, however, that a child's ability to interact positively and successfully with her peers is an important indication of social competence and adjustment in adult life.

If a child is not considered to be well-accepted by her peers, does this preclude her from having the ability or opportunities to have friends? According to John Gottman (1986), not necessarily. He notes that overall acceptance by the peer group and having a best friend are two separate and distinct issues. Children who are well-liked or accepted by everyone in their class may not have best friends in that group. On the other hand, children who are poorly accepted or disliked by most of their classmates can still have mutual friendships with peers. Gottman believes that parents' and teachers' concerns for the neglected or rejected child should be alleviated if that child has established a satisfying, pleasurable, and reciprocal friendship. Karly's and Henry's case provides a good illustration of two children who were likely neglected by most of their peers, yet established a solid best friendship that was beneficial to both and that relieved the concerns of their parents and teachers about their social adjustment.

What is the relationship between being well-accepted and having a best friend? Jeffrey Parker and Steven Asher (1993) substantiated the importance of friendship in a study they conducted to evaluate differences among friendships in low-, average-, and high-accepted children. They found that high-accepted children and average-accepted children were about twice as likely to have a very best friend as low-accepted children. But they also found that quite a few of the children identified as low-accepted did have friends, even when friendship was defined rigidly. Perhaps most importantly, they found that the children in their study without best friends were more lonely than children with best friends, regardless of how well-accepted they were by their peer group.

WHY ARE CHILDREN LONELY?

The research has clearly linked having friends, even just one special friend, with the reduction of loneliness in children and adults. Consequently, it should signal a red flag to parents and teachers if a child does not have any friends. Children can be without friends for many reasons: because of personal characteristics such as physical appearance, gender, or race, or situational factors such as opportunities for participation and mobility of the peer group (whether the children often work together as a group or are frequently separated) (Asher, Oden & Gottman, 1977). Difficulties in social skills are also an important contributor to difficulties in peer relationships. Because children with disabilities may look and act differently, exhibit poor social and communication skills, and experience limited opportunities to participate with their typically developing peers in community-wide contexts, it is quite likely that they will be without friends.

Other reasons children may have trouble making friends include being inhibited and exhibiting a great deal of nonsocial activity. These children often choose to play by themselves. Over time they may become locked within a cycle of social inhibition, leading to negative self-perceptions of social competence. This, in turn, leads to further withdrawal (Rubin, LeMare, & Lollis, 1990).

There are also other factors in a child's life that may contribute to her feelings of loneliness. These may include moving to a new school or neighborhood; losing an object, possession, or pet; losing a friend; experiencing conflict within the home or at school; or experiencing the death of a pet or a significant person (Bullock, 1993). These factors are more likely to be associated with "state" loneliness, the sense or feeling of loneliness caused by situational factors. Awareness of these causes is important so that intervention, such as counseling, can be provided before the "state" loneliness turns into "trait" loneliness, which can be persistent and long-lasting.

People's desire for company and their perceptions of relationships can both change from time to time. For example, people's feelings of loneliness increase when they feel badly about themselves as the result of some other cause such as doing poorly in school. Positive self-esteem is critical to the quality of everyone's life. In Lindsey's and Corrie's case, Lindsey's self-esteem was uplifted when she was given the opportunity to help someone else. Not only was she able to forge a true friendship with another child, but her reading abilities improved and her behavior problems significantly declined. Corrie's self-esteem was also bolstered as a result of her friendship with Lindsey. When Corrie was with Lindsey, she did not mumble, look down, or ignore her friend's questions, as she usually did with other children. Rather, she made eye contact, spoke in a loud, articulate voice, and appropriately acknowledged and responded to Lindsey's questions and conversations. Corrie's mother noticed the difference at home:

> This is the first time that Corrie has ever come home from school and expressed interest in having a friend sleep over. It's Lindsey this and Lindsey that. Lindsey called her the other night and my husband and I were truly amazed when Corrie spent more than five minutes in a conversation with her. We have to beg her to say more than two words when her grandmother calls.

Early on, Harry Sullivan (1953) claimed that friendship was an irreplaceable context for developing a child's empathy and perspective-taking skills and that friendships with peers serve to validate a child's interests, hopes, and positive self-perceptions. Sullivan predicated that, because a child's need for a friend develops later than her need for inclusion in a group, successful friendships with others might offset to some degree the negative effects of earlier difficulties in peer acceptance. Corrie's and Lindsey's friendship provides some evidence to this point. The lesson that their story gives us is that it is never too late to facilitate and support a child's opportunities to make friends, and that the adults in children's lives should never give up on nurturing friendships.

Loneliness and Children with Disabilities: What Does the Research Reveal?

The research on the loneliness of typically developing children has in large part been inspired by an extensive body of literature on loneliness in adolescence and adulthood. Not surprisingly, researchers have found that lonely adults often led lonely lives as children. As discussed above, there are many reasons to believe that children with disabilities are more likely to be without friends, thus leading them to loneliness in childhood and eventually adulthood. A better understanding of the limited body of research is critical to our understanding of the causes of loneliness among children, as well as the effects, so that we can consider appropriate means to prevent it.

The research on loneliness in children suggests that (Barthe & Park, 1993; Parkhurst & Asher, 1992; Renshaw & Brown, 1993):

- Children have a basic understanding of the concept of loneliness;
- A substantial number of children feel lonely;
- Feelings of loneliness can be measured reliably at different age levels;
- Feelings of loneliness are stable over a period of time;
- Low status in the peer group can result in greater feelings of loneliness and social dissatisfaction for young adolescents, children in middle childhood, and even among children as young as five and six.

How do these research findings translate to children with disabilities? In an early study, Jay Gottlieb and Yona Leyser (1981) found that children with developmental delays usually occupied the "lower" positions of their peer group, although they also found that not all children with disabilities were socially rejected. In fact, they concluded that whether a child with disabilities is able to make friends is partly determined by her individual traits and behaviors, just as it is for typically developing children.

Although many children with disabilities are actively rejected or ignored by their nondisabled peers, how acutely they feel such rejection is less known. Two possibilities exist. On the one hand, children with disabilities may not be aware of peer rejection due to deficits of social sensitivity and social insight. On the other hand, some children with disabilities tend to show reluctance and wariness in social situations, suggesting that they acutely feel their social rejection. Richard Luftig (1988) attempted to address this question. He attempted to measure "loneliness" among children with developmental disabilities and their same-age, typically developing peers. His study revealed that the students with developmental disabilities reported themselves to be more lonely than did their counterparts without disabilities. His conclusion was that if educational environments are to be least restrictive for children with disabilities, social skill intervention needs to become a part of the curriculum. I further maintain that friendships should be actively facilitated and maintained within all educational environments for *all* children.

Another study was designed to determine whether children with mild developmental delays understand the concept of loneliness, whether their feelings of loneliness at school can be reliably assessed, and whether there are differences in loneliness between children with and without disabilities. Three peer relationship variables to predict levels of loneliness were used: 1) low sociometric status in the peer group, 2) having no friends in class, and 3) having friendships that are relatively low in supportiveness. Because social skill deficits and peer rejection are associated with loneliness, feelings of loneliness may be especially prevalent among children with disabilities. The authors of this research found that the participants with disabilities understood the concept of loneliness; a high proportion of the children demonstrated that they knew what loneliness is and how to alleviate feelings of loneliness. Unfortunately, many of the participants also shared personal experiences of loneliness (Williams & Asher, 1992).

Richard Amado (1993) has addressed the issue of loneliness among adults with developmental disabilities and concludes that despite the substantial body of research on the effects of loneliness in the general population, the effects of loneliness on persons with disabilities who participate in the service system have not been thoroughly discussed. He points to the fact that human service practices for adults with disabilities have been slow to recognize their clients as total human beings rather than as the disabilities that make them eligible for services. In particular, the services themselves have been designed around fixing the resulting ills, rather than addressing the causes of loneliness or being redesigned to promote normal relationships and prevent loneliness in the first place. As Amado gives a call for social service agencies to take more responsibility surrounding issues of loneliness for adults with disabilities, the question remains: Whose responsibility is it to address the issue of loneliness among children?

Loneliness and Quality of Life: Effects on Children and Adults

Children who are isolated and who continually experience rejection are at a significant risk for academic failure, juvenile delinquency, school drop-out, and mental health concerns (Reisman, 1981). Children in elementary grades who are identified as lonely are less physically active than their nonlonely peers (Page, Frey, Talbert, & Falk, 1992). Adolescents who are lonely are more likely to use drugs, smoke cigarettes, practice unsafe weight loss procedures, and watch more television than their peers. In short, lonely, friendless, and/or isolated children are at risk to experience poor social learning opportunities and adjustment problems later in life that will contribute to poor emotional and physical well-being (Page, 1988).

The effects of loneliness on adults are even more negative and potentially deadly. For instance, heart-related illnesses and deaths are highly related to disruptions in an adult's interpersonal life such as the loss of a spouse and the lack of close family and community ties (Perlman & Peplau, 1982). Richard Amado (1993) concludes that loneliness is a "potentially aversive condition that creates a context for life that can promote personal conflict, emotional distress, poor health, antisocial and potentially dangerous behavior and premature death in the population at large" (pp. 75-76).

Loneliness in the Schools: Whose Responsibility?

Schools are among the greatest socialization settings in our culture and the most influential for shaping the course of human development over the life span. They are also one of the likeliest places for children to build friendships. Yet, as many as 20 to 30 percent of students experience substantial social adjustment problems in the classroom, putting them at risk for a variety of interpersonal, emotional, and career difficulties in later life (Ladd, 1990). During the first weeks of school, friendship serves as an important source of support for young children. Close times with classmates (e.g., friends) may serve as a "secure base" from which to explore and cope with new surroundings and demands. Children who form new friendships in their classroom also tend to gain in school performance over the course of the year. Children who do not make friends are most vulnerable to feelings of loneliness (Ladd, 1990).

Given that a child's participation in her school and classroom settings plays an important role in the development of her relationships with others, what are the factors that keep students from developing these important alliances? In an early book on loneliness in the schools, Robert Marc (1973) identified several factors that he felt kept students from building friendships at the classroom and school level. Alarmingly, these same factors are still present in many schools today. Marc's factors included:

- Static ability grouping;
- Age/grade placement that precludes students from developing positive relationships with older students or from developing responsibility for helping and modeling appropriate behavior for younger students;

- Isolation of children with disabilities;
- Physical organization of the school and class-room (lack of space for children to mingle with one another);
- Curricular and instructional separators such as overuse of worksheets and workbooks;
- Unfair competitive practices, report cards, and testing;
- Class rules that emphasize no talking in class, as well as do your own work;
- Lack of emphasis on socialization skills and on joint success endeavors;
- Adults/teachers who do not know enough about the student's world (pp. 12-37).

Fortunately, although the factors above are still present in many schools and classrooms, educators have built an impressive knowledge base of classroom best practices that are intentionally designed to foster and support children's friendships in academic environments. One of these strategies has been to implement more social skill building opportunities for children in the classroom setting. So-called loneliness intervention programs also now exist for both children and adults. Their major value lies in their ability to change lonely people's inappropriate friendship behavior and to redirect ineffective attitudes about the person's own value and esteem (Duck, 1991). Steve Duck suggests that when planning childhood loneliness interventions, it is useful for educators to understand that a sense of helplessness often accompanies loneliness. These feelings of loss of control may seriously impair an individual's ability to change aspects of loneliness in his life that he otherwise should be able to control. Duck recommends that educators develop strategies that foster a sense of learned hopefulness in children and adolescents, giving them the means of achieving perceived or actual control over their own lives.

When school staff are positively involved with each other, care about each other, work cooperatively, and plan together in the best interests of all their students, school communities will be better equipped to address issues of loneliness not only among their students, but also among their faculty and staff. Specific strategies in the classroom can also help reduce an individual child's sense of loneliness, particularly if he is welcomed and experiences a sense of belonging. In short, I maintain that schools accept responsibility for the well-being of all their students and this includes children who are "at-risk" because of loneliness. Since children with disabilities are often more vulnerable to loneliness in their lives, educators must be especially responsive to their need for friendships. Further strategies for developing friendships among children in classroom and school settings are addressed in Chapter 10.

A Story of Loneliness Continued

For two of their school years, Corrie and Lindsey each had a best friend with whom to hang out at recess, share lunch, and invite over for get-togethers. While Lindsey recognized that Corrie had a disability, she believed that her friendship with Corrie was "just the same as it would be for any other kids." Even though Corrie and Lindsey moved on to different classes in their fifth- and fourth-grade years respectively, they made a point of seeking each other out at recess and lunch. On the days that either girl was absent from school, the other was isolated and alone for that day. In addition to the companionship Lindsey and Corrie provided each other, other benefits of their relationship were noted. For example, I asked Lindsey's and Corrie's third-fourth grade teacher to share what he felt were the benefits of this relationship for each of the girls:

> I think Lindsey benefits from her relationship with
> Corrie because Lindsey can be herself and she doesn't
> worry that Corrie will judge her. Corrie is "safe" for
> Lindsey. Lindsey's self-esteem is up when she is around
> Corrie. She also really enjoys "helping" Corrie by
> reading to her, and she expresses pleasure at Corrie's

*growth as well. Corrie benefits from her friendship
with Lindsey because Lindsey responds to her needs,
laughs with her, hangs out with her. I think Lindsey is
Corrie's first friend. Having a relationship with a peer
is new to Corrie and I think she benefits from knowing
Lindsey accepts her for who she is. I find these two
similar in an odd sort of way. They both have trouble
letting people get too close. Yet with each other they
are very comfortable and nurturing.*

In her sixth-grade year, Corrie left Jane Austen Elementary to attend her neighborhood elementary school, Fir Crest. In fact, her fifth-sixth grade, general education teacher transferred to Fir Crest because it was closer to her home and insisted that Corrie make the move with her. The same year, Lindsey's family moved again to a small town about thirty miles away from Jane Austen. While Corrie's sixth-grade teacher, Mrs. Cassidy, made every effort to include Corrie as a fully participating member in her sixth-grade class, Corrie never developed the same type of friendship she had with Lindsey. Unfortunately, by the time she moved on to her first year in junior high school, an environment that did not focus on building friendship and membership opportunities for its students, Corrie was again friendless and isolated. She ate lunch alone, traveled between her classes alone, and was teased by her classmates in math and reading resource classes for her "quirky" behaviors. At the same time, Corrie's family was dealing with very serious issues at home that involved Corrie's older brother. Corrie's invisibility at school likely traveled with her to her home.

Lindsey called Corrie a couple of times from her new home and mentioned trying to get together with her. The get-together never happened and the girls eventually lost all contact with each other. Even before moving to her new school, Lindsey worried about making friends and whether her classmates would like her. She admitted to having a history of being "a pain in the butt" to new teachers in new situations and felt that this was one of the reasons she had difficulty making friends. Several months into Lindsey's new school year, I asked one of the special education teachers how she was doing. The behavior issues that had haunted Lindsey in the past had returned and she was having a lot of difficulty with academic subjects. I also asked whether Lindsey had made any friends. The special education teacher responded, "Well, I don't really pay too much attention to that kind of thing. But I haven't noticed her hanging out with any particular crowd or talking to me about anyone special. I don't really know."

Perhaps the greatest tragedy surrounding Corrie's and Lindsey's story of loneliness is the lack of attention and concern it drew from the significant adults in their lives. Too often it is the "overly social" child, the one who is constantly talking to her peers during class time or not completing her work because she is too socially engaged, who receives the attention (albeit, often negative) of their teachers. It is the withdrawn, isolated child who is easily overlooked, who becomes invisible. Yet the evidence so strongly speaks to the detrimental effects of loneliness among children, both with and without disabilities. By focusing on the negative outcomes that can occur for children who do not have friends, this chapter further illuminates the benefits of friendship highlighted in earlier sections of this book. Taken together, the evidence makes a compelling case for the need for schools to assume greater responsibility in addressing children's needs for friendship.

References

Amado, R.S. (1993). Loneliness: effects and implications. In A.N. Amado (Ed.), *Friendship and community connections between people with and without developmental disabilities* (pp. 67-84). Baltimore, MD: Paul H. Brookes.

Asher, S.R., Hymsel, S., & Renshaw, P.D. (1984). Loneliness in children. *Child Development, 55,* 1456-1464.

Asher, S.R., Oden, S.L., & Gottman, J.M. (1977). Children's friendships in school settings. In L.G. Katz (Ed.), *Current topics in early childhood education (Vol. 1).* Norwood, N.J.: Ablex Publishing.

Asher, S.R. & Renshaw, P.D. (1981). Children without friends: social knowledge and social skill training. In S.R. Asher & J.M. Gottman (Eds.), *The development of children's friendships.* New York, NY: Cambridge University Press.

Barth, J.M. & Parke, R.D. (1993). Parent-child relationship influences on children's transitions to school. *Merrill-Palmer Quarterly, 39,* 173-195.

Bullock, J.R. (1993). Children's loneliness and their relationships with family and peers. *Family Relations, 42,* 46-49.

Coleman, J.M., McHam, L.A., & Minnett, A.M. (1992). Similarities in the social competencies of learning disabled and low achieving elementary school children. *Journal of Learning Disabilities, 25 (10),* 671-677.

Duck, S. (1991). *Understanding relationships.* New York: The Guilford Press.

Gottlieb, J. & Leyser, Y. (1981). Friendship between mentally retarded and nonretarded children. In S.R. Asher & J.M. Gottman (Eds.), *The development of children's friendships.* New York, NY: Cambridge University Press.

Gottman, J.M. (1986). The world of coordinated play: Same and cross-sex friendships in young children. In J.M. Gottman & J.G. Parker (Eds.), *Conversations of friends: Speculations on affective development.* New York, NY: Cambridge University Press.

Hojat, M. & Crandall, R. (Eds.) (1989). *Loneliness: Theory, research and applications.* Newbury Park, CA: Sage Press.

Hymel, S. (1983). *Social isolation and rejection in children: The child's perspective.* Paper presented at the biennial meeting of the Society for Research in Child Development, Detroit.

Ladd, G.W. (1990). Having friends, keeping friends, making friends and being liked by peers in the classroom: Predictors of children's early school adjustment? *Child Development, 61,* 1081-1100.

Larson, R.W. (1990). The solitary side of life: An examination of the time people spend alone from childhood to old age. *Developmental Review, 10,* 155-183.

Luftig, R.L. (1985). *Correlates of children's loneliness.* Paper presented at the annual meeting of the American Education Research Association, Chicago, IL.

Luftig, R.L. (1988). Assessment of the perceived school loneliness and isolation of mentally retarded and nonretarded students. *American Journal on Mental Retardation, 92 (5),* 472-475.

Marc, R. (1973). *Loneliness in the schools (what to do about it).* Niles, Il: Argus Communications.

Page, R.M. (1988). Adolescent loneliness: A priority for school health education. *Health Education, 21 (5),* 20-21.

Page, R.M., Frey, J., Talbert, R., & Falk, C. (1992). Children's feelings of loneliness and social dissatisfaction: Relationship to measures of physical fitness and activity. *Journal of Teaching in Physical Education, 11,* 211-219.

Parker, J.G. & Asher, S.R. (1993). Friendship and friendship quality in middle childhood: Links with peer group acceptance and feelings of loneliness and social dissatisfaction. *Developmental Psychology, 29,* 611-621.

Parkhurst, J.T. & Asher, S.R. (1992). Peer rejection in middle school: Subgroup differences in behavior, loneliness and interpersonal concerns. *Developmental Psychology, 28 (2),* 231-241.

Perlman, D. & Peplau, L.A. (1982). Loneliness research: A survey of empirical findings. In L.A. Peplau & S.E. Goldstein (Eds.), *Preventing the harmful consequences of severe and persistent loneliness.* Rockville, MD: NIMH.

Ponzetti, J.J. (1990). Loneliness among college students. *Family Relations, 39 (3)* 336-340.

Reisman, J.M. (1981). Adult friendships. In S. Duck & R. Gilmour (Eds.), *Personal relationships, 2: Developing personal relationships.* London: Academic Press.

Renshaw, P.D. & Brown, P.J. (1993). Loneliness in middle childhood: Concurrent and longitudinal predictors. *Child Development, 64,* 1271-1284.

Rubin, K.H., LeMare, L.J., & Lollis, S. (1990). Social withdrawal in childhood: Developmental pathways to peer rejection. In S.R. Asher & J.D. Coie (Eds.), *Peer rejection in childhood.* New York, NY: Cambridge University Press.

Sullivan, H.S. (1953). *The interpersonal theory of psychiatry.* New York: W.W. Norton.

Weiss, S.R. (1982). Loneliness: What we know about it and what we might do about it. In L.A. Peplau & S.E. Goldstein (Eds.), *Preventing the harmful consequences of severe and persistent loneliness.* Rockville, MD: NIMH.

Williams, G.A. & Asher, S.R. (1992). Assessment of loneliness at school among children with mild mental retardation. *American Journal on Mental Retardation, 96 (4),* 373-385.

Chapter 8

Differences, Disability, & Adults:
Roadblocks to Friendship

"It is human nature to stand in the middle of a thing."
(Marianne Moore)

"Elections for student council will take place in the gym at this time for intermediate grades only. Please send your students in as soon as possible." Mr. Cosby, the principal at Jane Austen Elementary, makes his announcement and then quickly heads out to the hallway to greet the students as they enter the gymnasium. He shares a special "hello" or "hey, how's it going" with many of the students as they walk by. He catches Theresa's and Nelle's attention as they walk past and teases them, "Now, don't get too wild in there, girls." Theresa's face reddens slightly and she puts her hand over a giggle that threatens to escape. Nelle smiles bashfully at Mr. Cosby.

The girls join their fourth-, fifth-, and sixth-grade school mates in the loud, busy gymnasium. Posters intended to secure votes clutter the walls of the large room: "I'm the one to get the job done, vote Juan" and "You can count on Sam to be the man." Nelle and Theresa take a seat on the floor next to one of Theresa's friends, Sarah, from their fifth-sixth, multigrade class. The candidates make brief speeches meant to entice their constituents: more class parties, adjustable basketball hoops, better school lunches, and more exciting assemblies seem to top the list of promises being made. It appears that these young politicians have already learned to talk the talk!

Neither Theresa nor Nelle expresses much interest in the election process. Theresa spends most of her time whispering to Sarah, seated on her left. Nelle, seated on Theresa's right, yawns and plays with a small piece of trash she has found on the floor. The ballots are passed out so that students can vote. Theresa turns to Sarah and points to her ballot to indicate who she is voting for. Then she turns to Nelle, who is a nonreader, and tells her which candidate's name to put a mark next to. Theresa doesn't take time to read the names of the candidates to Nelle or express her opinion on them. Nelle seems baffled by the whole process but does what Theresa tells her. The same scenario plays out for the remainder of the voting process; Theresa and Sarah confer on who to vote for, giggling and laughing, and when the decision is made, Theresa leans over to Nelle and tells her, "Mark it here, Nelle." After the voting is completed, Sarah and Theresa leave the gym, their arms linked. Nelle doesn't move until Theresa looks behind her, notices Nelle's lack of movement, and calls after her in an annoyed voice, "Let's go, Nelle." Nelle slowly gets up and follows Theresa and Sarah back to their classroom.

Changes and Challenges

Nelle and Theresa have been "friends" since their third-grade year. Yet, it has become increasingly difficult to characterize their relationship as a friendship. Since the spring of their fifth-grade year and now two months into their sixth-grade year, there has been an increasing amount of tension in their interactions with each other. It is difficult to determine what has gone wrong with their friendship, which began with so much promise and provided so many benefits to both girls. But the root of their problems seems to lie in well-meaning, good-intentioned adults who have unknowingly created barriers and interruptions to the natural development of their friendship.

Research, practice, and common sense substantiate the importance of the adult role in nurturing learning and social outcomes for children with and without disabilities in the classroom. Teacher interest, a sense of ownership, and high expectations are known factors in the creation of an effective, child-centered classroom. As a matter of fact, these "best practices" are many of the same that will be addressed in Chapter 10. Nelle's and Theresa's fifth-sixth, multi-age class, taught by Mr. Howard, certainly met the standards of a high quality classroom. So how, when the best supports were in place, did Nelle's and Theresa's friendship deteriorate? There are several possible reasons to consider. First, was there a shift in their social development creating too big of a gap, as occurred in Karly's and Deanne's friendship? Or were Theresa and Nelle passing through the stages of friendship and had they come to the termination phase of their relationship? Either of these explanations could have been true. However, Theresa explained the problems in her friendship with Nelle in two sentences:

> If they [the adults in the classroom] had some problem
> with Nelle, they would always ask me to do something
> with her and it's sort of like I am her baby sitter now.
> But I just wanted to be her friend.

By most accounts, helping another person is a good thing. As a matter of fact, one of the primary functions of friendship is to provide help when it is needed. Aristotle, said by some to be the "father of friendship" (Bukowski & Sippola, 1996), believed that the goal of friendship is to do good for one's friend. Nelle's and Theresa's relationship was initiated on the basis of need and "goodness." The girls first met in their third-grade year when Nelle, a nonverbal child with moderate mental retardation, was included with her general education classmates for the first time. After noticing Nelle playing alone on the school playground, Theresa initiated contact with her. They connected immediately. A shy, quiet child at that time, Theresa felt Nelle needed a friend. Keeping in Jane Austen Elementary's tradition of moving from grade to grade in "families," they have been together in the same class for several years.

Friendships are also based on the idea of reciprocity, a concept that was covered in Chapter 5. Nelle and Theresa each benefited from their relationship in many ways. Both girls were lonely, shy, and excluded from the larger social network around them when they first met. Their friendship provided both with companionship and confidence.

A third potentially misunderstood parameter of friendship, expressed by Aristotle, is the notion of egalitarianism among partners. This is not to say that two individuals must be "equal" in terms of cognitive, social, or even emotional ability. Rather, a friendship that is "equal" is based on the recognition of "goodness in the other person and is characterized by virtue, kindness, benevolence, and justice" (p. 241, Bukowski & Sippola, 1996). Theresa's and Nelle's friendship showed signs of all of these characteristics.

When Nelle and Theresa first became friends, Theresa, a very bright student and gifted reader, was a self-proclaimed loner. In the classroom, she was viewed as a follower and a helper who was well-liked by her peers. At the time I first started observing Theresa's and Nelle's friendship, the girls were in fifth grade and Theresa was in the process of becoming more socialized with her classmates. Her teacher, Mr. Howard, described this change: "I'd say at the beginning of the year Theresa was an enabler. She was a person who took care of kids, took care of other people. Now she's hanging out with more of the girls in the class." Theresa's increasing membership in various social groups in the class was also noticed by a data collector who commented on Theresa's interactions with her classmates: "She is not a leader in her group by any means, but she does seem to be well-liked. It seems like she's along on the outside of the group looking in, trying to win their approval, but she is becoming more a part of the group all the time."

While Theresa's relationships with her classmates were growing and changing, her relationship with Nelle was also changing from what had begun as a friendly, companionable relationship to one that could be described as a "helping" relationship. Prior to their fifth-grade year, Nelle and Theresa were often found playing together at recess, looking at books together, and giggling quietly with one another as they walked hand in hand to the school buses at the end of the day. However, by the time the two girls were in fifth grade, many of their interactions involved Theresa helping Nelle with some type of task. Sometimes Theresa initiated the help and sometimes it was solicited by a teaching assistant, the classroom teacher, or Nelle herself, as illustrated in the following examples:

> The teacher asked the class to come over and sit on the carpet. Theresa put her hand on Nelle's shoulder, leaned over, and said something to her. The teaching assistant asked Theresa to help Nelle with her math. Theresa asked Nelle if she would like some help. Nelle nodded "yes" and they began to work on problems using the calculator.
>
> Theresa went over to Nelle, put her hand on her shoulder, and asked if she could correct her math for her. "Gosh Nelle! Look at that!" Theresa said in a quiet, excited voice. She finished correcting all of the problems and told Nelle quietly, "You got them all right."

Theresa's ability to understand and relate to Nelle was no doubt an important reason why their relationship evolved from a friendly, companionable one to a helping one. One of the data collectors for this research summed it up as follows:

I think that it is assumed by the others in the class
[teaching assistant, teacher, and students] as well as
by Theresa, that she is responsible for helping Nelle.
Theresa knows Nelle very well. She knows what she
likes and what she doesn't like, and she can explain
why she is behaving the way she is.

Theresa's and Nelle's teacher, Mr. Howard, was also quite aware of Theresa's ability to understand Nelle: "If I think that Nelle isn't understanding what's going on, I can always count on Theresa to explain it to her, to help her to better understand what we're doing."

At the same time that Theresa's and Nelle's relationship was changing from a friendly one to a "helping" one, Theresa also started to grow apart from Nelle as she began to develop friendships with more of the students in their class. Mr. Howard recognized this change: "I think that Theresa is moving in and out of friendship circles in the class. Sometimes Nelle is included (although often on a very artificial level) and sometimes she isn't included at all." Furthermore, Theresa started showing signs that she resented her relationship with Nelle, as illustrated in this observation:

Nelle kept working on her math. The teaching assistant
asked, "Theresa, are you going to help Nelle with her
math?" Theresa replied, "She . . . she keeps punching in
the numbers wrong on her calculator and I told her but
she wouldn't change it so I'm not going to help her now."

Theresa was aware of her conflicting feelings toward Nelle and the shift that was occurring in their relationship. Her newly formed friendships with other classmates also created stress in her long-standing commitment to Nelle and her desire to be accepted and liked by her peers, as reflected in this comment:

"Well, if she [Nelle] can't find something or do something she always comes to me. Sometimes I just want to hang out with my friends. Sometimes it really annoys me." A data collector who spent many hours observing Theresa's and Nelle's friendship also noticed the conflict: "Theresa's relationship with Nelle looks very different than her relationship with other students in the class. She helps Nelle with her work and mothers her while she looks to her group of friends for friendship and acceptance."

Nelle was also going through changes herself. Like many of her peers, Nelle was beginning to enter adolescence, a period of time typically associated with a growing need for independence. Nelle's parents had always been conservative in their views with regard to raising their two daughters, Nelle and her older sister, Jeannette. Although Nelle had a very limited vocabulary, her communication was clear: she did not want to be treated like a baby. She was no longer content to allow her mother to pick out her clothes or do her hair. In an interview during the spring of Nelle's fifth-grade year, her mother expressed her concern over Nelle's recent assertiveness: "This is very difficult for us at home. Nelle is constantly arguing with us regarding anything we suggest. 'No, no, no,' she'll say. Jeannette, who is older by three years, has never given us any difficulties even as a teenager." Nelle's new sense of independence was also spilling over to the classroom. Because Nelle had always been so compliant and willing to please in the past, the adults in the classroom, as well as many of her classmates, weren't sure how to handle this change in her personality. Unfortunately, rather than nurturing this growth in Nelle, the adults and several of her peers, including Theresa, tried to reshape Nelle back to the compliant and willing girl they knew and were comfortable with.

Theresa may have been content and even happy to support Nelle's new growth in independence. But, as mentioned earlier, she was receiving more and more pressure from the adults in the classroom, including Mr. Howard and the teaching assistants who worked with Cole and Nelle, to take care of Nelle. Before the end of their fifth-grade year, Theresa had become Nelle's "designated care taker." Mr. Howard and the teaching assistants, challenged by supporting a classroom of thirty students, two of whom had moderate and severe mental retardation, began to rely on the typically developing children to help their friends with disabilities. Naturally, the students who were most "connected" to the child with disabilities, as Theresa was to Nelle, became the ones who were counted on the most to help out.

Nelle's and Theresa's friendship is a good case example of the different meanings that adults and typically developing children have with regard to their relationships with a peer with disabilities. While Mr. Howard and the teaching assistants were supportive of and pleased by Nelle's and Theresa's friendship, they seemed to view the connection that the girls shared as a useful resource for instruction and classroom management. Perhaps Mr. Howard's reliance on Theresa as an instructional assistant for Nelle illustrates one of the many dilemmas that teachers in inclusive classrooms face: balancing the competing needs and limited resources that are available to them in these settings. Mr. Howard and the other significant adults in Nelle's and Theresa's lives may not have viewed the role of helper as different from the role of a friend, yet Theresa clearly recognized the difference. Indeed, this is one area in the literature on inclusive schooling and social relationships that has received very little attention. The development of natural friendships between children with and without disabilities, and the role of "help" in these relationships, has not been adequately addressed.

"The Politics of Help" and What It Means to Friendship

Emma Van der Klift and Norman Kunc (1994), two of the first advocates to underscore the importance of understanding the "politics of help" and its effect on individuals with disabilities, devoted a chapter to this very issue. They stated:

At the end of the 20th century, the most significant
barriers preventing individuals with labels of disability
from fully participating in schools and communities
are still attitudinal. Our society still perceives those
with disabilities as perpetual receivers of help. Descrip-
tors such as "less fortunate" and "needy" telethons, and
tear-jerker journalism all continue to perpetuate this
view (p. 392).

Furthermore, while Van der Klift and Kunc agree that it is
often essential that students be provided with formalized opportunities to interact, such as through classroom friendship
and support circles, overemphasizing the "helper-helpee" relationship between children with and without disabilities can
easily skew the delicate balance of giving and receiving that is
a critically important parameter of friendship. They don't deny
that help-giving contact may reduce an initial sense of strange-
ness or fear that some typically developing children may feel
toward their peers with disabilities and that it may lay the
groundwork for future friendship between children. However,
they adamantly argue that it is essential to acknowledge that
help is not and can never be the basis of friendship. The reciprocity between friends is what makes a friendship authentic.

The implication of Van der Klift's and Kunc's argument
is that teachers and parents must remember the unique and
almost magical aspects of friendship. Friendships cannot be
conjured up at will. Friendship is about choice, chemistry, and
reciprocal attraction between two individuals. While adults do
have influence over the nature of proximity and they can create and foster environments that promote the development of
potential friendships between children, we are not "friendship
sorcerers." Admittedly, sometimes people with disabilities do
need help. However, Van der Klift and Kunc warn, "If they are
uncomfortable receiving it [help], as many of us are, they are
left in a classic 'no win' position for either doing without help
or enduring the underlying demeaning messages" (p. 394).
Consequently, teachers and parents must examine the nature

of the interactions that they facilitate between and among children. We need to look closely at the role of help in the classroom, asking not whether children should help each other, but rather how that help takes place. One way to ensure that help is being offered properly is to remember to value and respect the diversity that exists among our children and students.

VALUING DIVERSITY: EASIER SAID THAN DONE?

Mr. Howard, Theresa's and Nelle's teacher, strived to value each and every one of his students. His goal was to create a classroom community that promoted belonging and acceptance for all. He did not rely on competition and stratification to provide his students with a sense of worth. Rather, he used cooperative learning strategies, project-based activities, and literature to promote collaboration and a high sense of self-esteem among his students. Mr. Howard's stress on literature was evident in his classroom, which was overflowing with books and reading materials for all levels of ability. When the students in his class were not engaged in independent expert studies or working on small group projects, they could be found in a large group discussing topics of current interest. The following excerpt from my observation notes was typical of group interactions in Mr. Howard's class:

> The students sat around the carpet, some on chairs . . .
> a few kids were sharing chairs and some sat on the
> floor or leaned on the table. Mr. Howard said, "So,
> what are you reading?" and they talked about the
> stories they were reading. They talked about "Go Ask
> Alice" and others. Mr. Howard asked one boy what
> moves a book from being scary to gory and they talked
> about the description of some things in the book. He
> asked another student what he looks for when he reads
> poetry. They continued the discussion and the kids
> listened well.

Mr. Howard certainly incorporated the right ingredients needed to build a classroom community that valued diversity among his students. He was very intent upon making sure that there was plenty of "conversation around the inclusion of students with disabilities in his classroom." Consequently, the majority of Mr. Howard's students were comfortable in the presence of Cole and Nelle and went out of their way to make sure that they participated and were included in the classroom activities. Unfortunately, through the process of ensuring that each individual child was valued and respected as unique in Mr. Howard's classroom, the focus on Nelle began to be centered on her disability. Mr. Howard, motivated by his own interest in the subject of how and why mental retardation occurs, spent time with his class reviewing the medical aspects of having a cognitive disability. The upshot was that Mr. Howard and his adult teaching assistants unconsciously interfered with the natural development of relationships for Nelle by paying so much attention to her disability. Emma Van der Klift and Norman Kunc (1994) warn that if we commend and praise typically developing children for their interactions with their peers with disabilities (either publicly or in other ways), we inadvertently make friendship a big deal and imply that all children are not created equal. They suggest that by making friendship between children with and without disabilities a big deal, "we reinforce the idea that it is morally and socially admirable to 'help the handicapped' and therefore may remove the opportunity for equality and reciprocity" (p. 397).

"HELPING" IS IN THE EYE OF THE BEHOLDER

Theresa, who had already developed a friendship with Nelle prior to entering Mr. Howard's class, was no doubt torn by the mixed messages she was receiving from the adults around her. On the one hand, Theresa was being praised and complimented for her "friendship with Nelle" and was finding that adults frequently relied on her to "help" Nelle. On the other hand, Theresa was feeling uncomfortable with this unnatural attention toward a friendship she had with another child. In some ways, it makes sense that she would begin to develop new friendships with typically developing classmates because these friendships were "no big deal."

If the growing change in their relationship was confusing for Theresa, it was probably just as upsetting if not more so for Nelle. Receiving help, some studies have found, can damage an individual's self-esteem and feelings of autonomy and self-worth. Help that is offered or help given can, under certain circumstances, "highlight the recipient's relative inferiority and lead to negative effects and unfavorable recipient self-evaluations" (Nadler & Mayseless, 1983). In short, Nelle had always experienced a balanced, give-and-take relationship with Theresa. When Theresa began assuming responsibility for Nelle and "helping" her, the balance was shifted. Nelle, as mentioned earlier, was going through some significant developmental changes with regard to her independence. Theresa's new care-taking role frustrated and upset Nelle as well. There are several examples in the observation notes from late in their fifth-grade year and throughout their sixth-grade year when Theresa initiated help toward Nelle and Nelle rejected it. By the end of their sixth-grade year, the girls had almost ceased all interactions with each other.

Fostering Friendships, Naturally

Creating classroom communities that promote belonging and acceptance for all is the first step toward facilitating friendships among children. But this is not necessarily enough, as Nelle's and Theresa's story revealed. A further task for teachers is to create the space in which relationships can develop by consciously thinking about and working on the nature of proximity. Van der Klift and Kunc (1994) present six ideas to assist the process:

1. ***Do not make friendship a big deal.*** As suggested earlier, allow friendships to follow a natu-

ral course of development. If too much attention is spent admiring the typically developing child for befriending a child with disabilities, we reinforce the idea of "helping the handicapped."

2. *Respect personal boundaries.* Van der Klift and Kunc remind us that boundaries of touch that would not be crossed between typically developing children should not be crossed with their classmates with disabilities. They suggest that an unfortunate side effect of benevolent interaction is a tendency to treat the child with disabilities like a life-size doll or pet or even a classroom mascot with whom the usual physical boundaries of touch may be violated. They recommend asking ourselves often, "Do the interactions between children in any way compromise the dignity of the individual with the disability?" (p. 398).

3. *Model behavior.* If teachers and other adults in the classroom treat all students with respect and dignity, their students will follow their cues. Obviously the same piece of advice goes for parents. Actions do speak louder than words.

4. *Encourage reciprocity and contribution.* According to Van der Klift and Kunc (1994): "When disability is seen as the largest component of a person, much of what is unique and 'human' about him or her will be obscured. When needs and deficits are what we see, we only see what the person cannot do" (p. 398). Consequently, we must recognize and acknowledge the diverse contributions that all individuals make. The main purpose of Chapter 5 was to highlight the reciprocal contributions that each child, with and without disabilities, made to their friendship. The focus shifted away from disability and towards a better understanding of the unique gifts that each child brought to their friendship.

5. *Merge respect and help.* One of the biggest
   challenges that teachers face in inclusive classrooms is getting other kids to stop doing everything for the child with a disability. However, if
   teachers step back and carefully evaluate their
   own behavior, they may very well find that their
   expectations for the child with disabilities are not
   high enough. Raising expectations on the part of
   both adults and the typically developing students
   in the classroom will lead to greater respect.
   Furthermore, help should always be natural and
   situation-rooted (Wright, 1983) and should be
   offered as "necessary help," not help that is artifi-
   cially contrived (Ladieu, Hanfmann, & Dembo
   cited in Wright, 1983, p. 310). Finally, we must
   listen to both the verbal and nonverbal messages
   expressed by someone who may or may not want
   help and teach our students to do this as well.
   Developing classroom norms where one checks out
   whether help or support is wanted will enhance
   the probability that help is offered under conditions of acceptance and respect (Bryant, 1997).

6. *Emphasize empathy and social justice.*
   Finally, Van der Klift and Kunc (1994) suggest
   that most children are acutely conscious of what
   is fair and what is not. Consequently, we must
   be careful not to accidentally reinforce the
   notion that those who have disabilities are
   objects of pity since equitable relationships
   cannot be built on a foundation of sympathy.
   Rather, we should strive to build relationships
   upon shared experiences and shared stories that
   create a sense of empathy, a sense of "I know
   what you mean." The authors caution that doing
   this does not disregard people's different experiences, but when experiences do intersect, an
   opportunity is presented for building connection

and understanding that may extend to other situations in unexpected ways.

Nelle and Theresa: A Bittersweet Ending?

Although Nelle's and Theresa's friendship took a different course than either of the girls may have desired, it still provided them with companionship, confidence, and a sense of community for several years. While their friendship had pretty much ended by the completion of their sixth-grade year, Theresa still had strong feelings for Nelle and worried about her adjustment to junior high school the following year:

> Yeah, you know next year Nelle is going to a different junior high than I am. I hope that the kids there like her and stuff. Since she doesn't talk real well they are going to have to figure out how to use her communication book and everything.

Nelle and Theresa got together once over the summer before moving on to new junior highs, but this was likely due less to a request from either girl and more to their parents' desire to socialize with each other. They too had gotten friendly with each other through the course of their daughters' relationship. I visited Nelle several times at the new junior high school and was pleased to see that she had made some friendly relationships with other students. Part of her ability to make friends with other children could no doubt be attributed to her experiences in her long-term friendship with Theresa. When I visited Nelle at her new school, I often asked her if she remembered her friends from Jane Austen Elementary whom she hadn't seen in awhile. Nelle responded enthusiastically to my queries by opening her communication book and pointing excitedly to her picture of Theresa. Just as Nelle had made an important contribution to Theresa's childhood, so had Theresa to Nelle's.

While the adults in their lives may also have wished for a different outcome to Nelle's and Theresa's story, their friendship raised some important issues to consider regarding friendships between children with and without disabilities. First, is it fair to ask typically developing children to take on the role of tutor or caretaker for their classmates with disabilities? If so, will they be given the opportunity to communicate their dissatisfaction, discomfort, or unpreparedness for this role? Second, how does the role of helper or caretaker affect the relationships between teacher, student without disabilities, and student with disabilities? Finally, considering respect and value for individual diversity and ability level, how much "help" should adults expect typically developing students to provide their peers with disabilities and how should this help be structured so that a balance is provided between giving and taking?

While we are only just beginning to address these questions, their importance becomes much more evident the more we learn about the delicate friendships that exist between children with and without disabilities. The following chapters will hopefully serve as a beginning guide toward understanding how to encourage and facilitate these important relationships in our children's lives.

References

Bryant, B.K. (in press). Children's coping at school: The relevance of failure and cooperative learning for enduring peer and academic success. In L.H. Meyer, H.S. Park, I.S. Schwartz, M. Grenot-Scheyer, & B. Harry (Eds.), *Understanding the social lives of children and youth with diverse abilities: The role of culture and development*. Baltimore, MD: Paul H. Brookes.

Bukowski, W.M. & Sippola, L.K. (1996). Friendship and morality: (How) are they related? In W.M. Bukowski, A.F. Newcomb, & W.W. Hartup (Eds.), *The company they keep: Friendship in childhood and adolescence*. New York, NY: Cambridge University Press.

Nader, A. & Mayseless, O. (1983). Recipient self-esteem and reactions to help. In J.D. Fisher, A. Nadler, & B.M. DePaulo (Eds.), *New directions in helping. Vol. 2: Recipient reactions to help*. New York: Academic Press.

Van der Klift, E. & Kunc, N. (1994). Beyond benevolence: Friendship and the politics of help. In J.S. Thousand, R.A. Villa, & A. Nevin (Eds.), *Creativity and collaborative learning: A practical guide to empowering students and teachers*. Baltimore, MD: Paul H. Brookes.

Wright, B.A. (1983). *Physical disability: A psycho-social approach* (2nd ed.). New York: Harper & Row.

PART III

The Significance of Meaning, Context, and Adult Support

Chapter 9

Family & Culture:
Influences on Friendships

"What its children will become, that will the community become."
(Suzanne Lafollette)

The weather was brutal on the April afternoon that I had scheduled an interview with Stacy's mother, Linda, regarding her typically developing daughter's friendship with Molly, a girl with disabilities. It isn't unusual to get rain, and lots of it in the Pacific Northwest, but this day was particularly wild. Loud claps of thunder followed bright, sharp streaks of lightning. The wind was blowing up gusts of 30 to 40 miles an hour as the rain beat in pellets against my office window. I considered rescheduling the interview, but was hesitant to do so. Pinning down this precious hour with Linda had been challenging—between her work as an instructional aide at Jane Austen Elementary, her two daughters' extracurricular events, and the many hours she volunteered at their school, I was lucky to secure this time.

Although I had met Linda once or twice before and had seen her around the school, I hadn't yet formed any solid impressions of her. On that cold, wet, windy day, Linda breezed into my office exactly at the scheduled time, shook the rain off the bright red umbrella which matched her red trench coat, ran a hand through her unmussed hair, and gave me a confident smile. My impression right then was of a woman who could handle anything and with grace, elegance, and charm.

I began my interview with Linda by asking her a general question, "Please describe Stacy for me." I continued through my protocol of questions, the same that I use with all of the parents of the typically developing children that I interview: I ask about their child's school history and their experiences in an inclusive school. I ask what they think or feel about their child's relationship with a peer with disabilities and what meanings or possible outcomes they think this friendship provides for their child. Next, I ask about any concerns or worries they might have concerning their child's friendship with a peer with disabilities. Finally, I ask the parents to share their feelings about inclusion, their own experiences with people who have intellectual disabilities, and what they would describe as the positive and negative aspects of inclusive education.

Linda was open and forthcoming during our interview. She shared the story of how Molly and Stacy first met (see Chapter 2), and what her feelings were regarding their friendship. Her responses to my queries were positive and enthusiastic. My initial impression of Linda as a confident, secure woman was reinforced as the interview went on. When I got to the "worries or concerns" section of the interview, I was expecting the usual response: that there might not always be enough support or resources for the inclusion of students with disabilities, or some children with disabilities might be too distracting for the other students and so on. Instead, Linda shared an incident that had occurred during the first year of

Stacy's friendship with Molly to reveal what had worried her most, her own fears:

> About six months into their second-grade year to-
> gether, Stacy must have asked me a dozen times if
> Molly could come over and play. I had so many excuses
> why Molly couldn't come over—dance practice, piano
> lessons, Molly lives too far away, etc., etc. Finally, after
> Stacy's persistence, I called Molly's mother. I was quite
> embarrassed, but I just blurted out, "You know, Stacy
> really wants Molly to come over and play, but what
> does she eat? What do I do if she chokes? What if she
> wants to go home? Does she know how to use the
> toilet? Will she be okay being away from home?" You
> know, Debbie, our generation is just so ignorant about
> these things. I was terrified the first time Molly came
> over to play. Well, it took all of about ten minutes to
> put my worries to rest. Molly was really just another
> kid—nothing secret, nothing surprising.

In spite of Linda's initial fears and concerns, Stacy's and Molly's friendship flourished. As Linda pointed out so frankly, having relationships, let alone friendships with people who have intellectual disabilities, is a new concept for most adults in our generation. Besides Linda, several other parents of typically developing children I interviewed referred to this fact. During their childhood, individuals with mental retardation were "hidden away," "segregated," and "seldom seen." So what does a parent's history and experience with disabilities mean for a child who has a friendship with someone who has disabilities? One thing that it means is that this generation of parents lacks a reference point of experience to share with their children regarding these unique friendships. Yet parents, families, and their cultural backgrounds, values, and beliefs are all known to greatly influence how children make and keep friends. If Linda had shared her early fears about Molly with her impressionable 7-year-old daughter, the outcome of Stacy's and Molly's relationship may well have turned out very differently.

Family and Cultural Influences on the Social Lives of Children with and without Disabilities

HOW DO PARENTS INFLUENCE THEIR CHILDREN'S FRIENDSHIPS?

"It is a truism that the life course of any individual is deeply affected by the beliefs, perspectives and planning of one's parents," states Beth Harry, an educational researcher, professor, and parent. Not surprisingly, social skills development is an area where parents carry great influence. According to Paul Mussen and Nancy Eisenberg-Berg (1977), parents are ordinarily the earliest and most significant agents of socialization. Because parents make the greatest contribution to their child's socialization and the personal characteristics acquired, social behaviors learned in the family setting are enduring and resistant to change.

There are many parental practices that will potentially affect a child's social life. They include: early child-rearing practices, discipline measures, physical and emotional nurturance, giving of praise and approval, giving or withholding love and material rewards, giving explanations and examples of rules, and how the parents model or demonstrate their own social behaviors. Mussen and Eisenberg-Berg (1977), researchers in the field of children's social behavior, conclude that parental modeling plays a major role in the development of a child's social behavior.

Parents also play a critical role in their child's moral development. A child's sense of moral obligation is related to her ability to make lasting and healthy friendships with peers. Steven Duck (1991) suggests that parents who devote energy to creating a favorable self-image in their young child are also laying the foundation for her future success with social relationships and moral development. For example, encouraging young children to notice their successful interactions with adults and other children, Duck notes, is one useful way of protecting and improving their self-image, thus enhancing successful future relationships.

When young children begin to play with one another, they are typically under the supervision of an adult, often a parent. During these interactions, their play and activities are to a large extent restricted, constrained, and supervised, usually for good reasons. Once they get old enough to be "independent initiators of play," how they interact with friends also changes. But their desires for friendship and social contact will have been shaped in large part by their level of self-esteem (Duck, 1991).

A large body of research also suggests that emotional as well as physical nurturance and affection are required if children are to develop positive relationships with others. However, Ervin Staub (1996), who has long studied the issue of caring among children, believes that sufficient nurturing isn't enough. He believes that children require guidance in their interactions with others and suggests that explaining reasons for rules to children is a positive form of guidance. Staub (1996) feels that one form of reasoning that is important in developing caring in children is "induction," which refers to pointing out to children the impact of their behaviors on others. For example, when a young child takes a toy away from a peer without asking and that peer begins to cry, the teacher can explain to the child why taking away the toy made the other child sad.

The parent's beliefs—especially the mother's—about friendship are also important in shaping a child's social life. Kenneth Rubin and his colleagues (Rubin, Mills, Rose-Karsnor, 1988) have shown that a mother's beliefs are directly related to her actual efforts to teach her children to be sociable. If the mother thinks that a friendship ought to "just happen," then she isn't likely to intercede if her child does not have friends. But if the mother thinks her child needs help, then she will encourage, support, and provide opportunities for her child to learn about friendship and to develop appropriate social skills.

Parents and other adults in children's lives are faced with
a dilemma when deciding how much influence they should have
on children's friendships. On the one hand, parents and teachers may believe that friends are a child's special domain and
that they shouldn't interfere. And indeed, as illustrated in the
previous chapter, too much adult interference can lead to the
end of a friendship, as was the case in Nelle's and Theresa's
relationship. On the other hand, parents are the ones who often choose and organize the settings, including neighborhoods
and schools, that enable children to meet one another. Zack
Rubin, author of *Children's Friendships* (1980), provides this
thought for parents to ponder:

> Our own values about friendships, whether they
> should be formal or informal, inclusive or exclusive,
> deep or superficial, are unmistakably conveyed to our
> children through the examples we set in our relation-
> ships with others. Thus, we cannot help influencing
> our children. We can only try to exert this influence
> wisely and thoughtfully, with a clear view of the
> special place of friendships in each child's life (p. 134).

HOW DOES CULTURE INFLUENCE CHILDREN'S FRIENDSHIPS?

Our cultural and ethnic histories and identities also influence our beliefs and practices and who we are as individuals, family members, and parents. In fact, the way we raise
our children is influenced by our cultural background and beliefs. Thus, it is not possible or reasonable to separate out the
differences between parental influences and cultural influences
on children's friendships. Rather, it makes more sense to view
them as interrelated factors. In addition, Beth Harry suggests
that "we learn that to recognize diversity is to see that culture
is but one of the innumerable threads that weave inextricably
through an individual's life experience. Competing or comple-
mentary threads include social class, education, language, gen-

der, disability, immigration status, and acculturational status, to mention only a few" (p. 48, 1998).

In order to have a discussion on cultural influences, it is first necessary to define what culture means. I have always found the following to make a lot of sense: "One way to define culture is to say that it is everything that makes up the life of a people—the objects they use in daily life, the ways they conduct their lives (that is, their customs), and the deep-seated and often unconscious reasons they do things in a certain way (their values)" (Williams and DeGaetana, 1985, p. 17).

Between parental influences and all the complexities of cultural influences, understanding the influences on children's friendships can be an unpredictable process. Yet, anthropologists have studied and described the norms of behaviors such as perceptions, cognitions, thoughts, beliefs, ideals, and values that are "expected" of people in particular cultures and subcultures for many years. Through their work and the cross-cultural data that they have collected, they conclude that the culture in which a child is reared is a major force in shaping her socialization skills.

Eleanor Lynch (1992), who co-authored a book on developing cross-cultural competence for early childhood educators, suggests that the influence of culture, language, and ethnicity is always easier to see in other people than in ourselves. Culture becomes like a second skin—we become so accustomed to our beliefs that we cease to notice that they exist. However, she believes that when we are out of touch with our own culture and its influence on us, it is difficult to work or relate effectively with people whose cultures differ from our own. Dr. Lynch suggests that "only when we examine the values, beliefs and patterns of behavior that are a part of our own cultural identity can we distinguish truth from tradition" (p. 21).

By most standards, such as socioeconomic status, ethnicity, language, level of education, etc., we would describe Stacy's and Molly's families as coming from similar cultural backgrounds. However, one of the major differences that these two families faced was that one family had a child with a disability and one did not. In some small way, Linda experienced a sense of "culture shock." The presence of a child with a disability in Molly's family was one of the many factors that characterized who Molly's family was, what their values and beliefs were based on, and how they behaved and interacted with others. Having a child with a disability was not a part of Linda's cultural experience, belief, and value system. When she invited Molly to her home, in some ways she was practicing a form of cross-cultural understanding. Lynch (1992) states:

> Achieving cross-cultural competence requires that we lower our defenses, take risks and practice behaviors that may feel unfamiliar and uncomfortable. It requires a flexible mind, an open heart, and a willingness to accept alternative perspectives. It may mean setting aside some beliefs that are cherished to make room for others whose value is unknown, and it may mean changing what we think, what we say, and how we behave" (p. 35).

"A POSTURE OF UNDERSTANDING"—INCREASING CROSS-CULTURAL COMPETENCE

Unfortunately, a thorough description of what we know about friendships across different cultures would encompass the rest of this chapter, if not this book. Given the focus of this book, a discussion about the influences of culture and family perspectives on children with disabilities and about increasing our own cultural understanding is more in line with the purposes of this chapter. Not surprisingly, little is written about friendships between children with and without disabilities who also experience different ethnic identities, language, or other cultural differences.

Recently, however, Beth Harry (1997) has sought to gain a better understanding of the differences in cultural patterns between American-born and foreign-born families who have children with disabilities. Over a period of four years, she and her colleagues worked closely with seven families of diverse social and cultural backgrounds whose common experience was the presence of a child with disabilities. Four of the families Dr. Harry spent time with had emigrated to the United States from El Salvador, the Dominican Republic, Palestine, and Trinidad. Of the three remaining American-born families, two were African-American, and one included a father who was third generation Chinese-American and a mother who was Caucasian American. The families also represented wide diversity in socioeconomic status. Dr. Harry found that despite obvious cultural variations, it was the special status of the child with the disability that brought out the shared longing for a "normal life" for their children across the seven families.

Dr. Harry concludes her chapter by stating this: "Regardless of culture, it seems true to say that the fact of the child's disability was a centerpiece in the family dynamics. Nevertheless, cultural influences were clearly discernible in variations among the families, and their presence indicates the need for American professionals who subscribe to mainstream values, to become sensitive to the discrepancies that might separate them [cultural influences] from families" (p. 58, 1998). Harry believes that a key to developing awareness and sensitivity to differences among people might be to take a "posture of understanding." This means that we seek mutual learning and understanding, despite the continuing presence of privately held opinions. Harry states that while we may still prefer our own system, if we can at least understand the underpinnings of a different belief system, then we can begin to feel and show, rather than simply simulate, respect for it.

Franz Boas (1943), an anthropologist, was one of the first to introduce the idea of understanding the thoughts of another group in an attempt to analyze their experience in terms of their concepts rather than our own. Basically, his suggestion was to try to see the world from a different point of view. If parents, families, and other adults significant in children's lives can use a "posture of understanding" when supporting the friendships between children with and without disabilities, the differences that exist between the children and their families will not be ignored or swept away, but rather acknowledged, discussed, and celebrated.

Families and Disabilities: Increasing Understanding and Sensitivity

FAMILIES WITH CHILDREN WITH DISABILITIES: CAREGIVING, STRESS, AND SUPPORT

Parenting can be challenging, stressful, demanding, and exhausting, even in the best of circumstances. Imagine, then, raising a child who is nonverbal, or who still needs help with toileting at age 12, or who is isolated and friendless, or who requires tube feeding or ongoing seizure supervision, or who needs an expensive and underinsured device like a wheelchair for mobility, or whose life expectancy has been pessimistically determined by every physician the parents have met with. These are only a few of the many challenges that parents and families with children with severe and multiple disabilities may face. Yet, in spite of these challenges, most of which are very different than for other parents and families, many of the dreams and visions that parents of children with disabilities have for their children are universally felt by all parents.

Jeff and Cindy Strully (1993), parents of a daughter who has severe mental retardation, write about what they have learned so far during their daughter's eighteen-year journey in life: "We have learned that the journey starts with a dream, desirable futures are possible, friendships are at the heart of any desirable future, and friendships can and should be nurtured and supported" (p. 217). They feel that a lesson they have gained from successes in facilitating friendship for children is that assistance is required. They also note that helping to facilitate friendship for their daughter has not always been a happy experience. They have experienced pain, frustration, and anger. When asked why they work so hard on friendship, often at the cost of everything else, such as competency or skill building for their daughter, they believe the answer is simple: "Without friendships in Shawntell's life, gaining additional skills and competencies is useless. Shawntell will be at increased risk of abuse, neglect, and exploitation without friends and relationships in her life" (p. 223).

In their work with families who have children with disabilities, Barb Buswell and Beth Schaffner (1990) have found that parents have a vision of what they want for their children's lives: "The vision begins by having all children learn side-by-side in an integrated classroom to ensure that they all have the skills and experiences necessary to live together in the community" (p. 219). They also found that parents who have the vision of "full inclusion" for their children must often become the pioneers and help guide the educational system through the necessary changes to make inclusive schooling possible. Diane Ryndak (1996) writes about collaboration with family and friends for meaningful education programs in inclusive settings and suggests that the use of proactive measures can allow school personnel to facilitate the active participation of family and other members of a child's support network. Ryndak (1996) defines a natural support network as: "the set of individuals with whom a person has ongoing interactions in everyday life, reflecting various levels of friendship, caring, support, and assistance for both parties across a variety of activities" (p. 62). Ryndak believes that using proactive measures can help overcome families' barriers to their participation, which might include:

1. language and communication problems;
2. differences in perceptions, attitudes, and values; and
3. logistical difficulties.

What are some of the proactive measures that families who have children with disabilities can take to ensure a quality education for *all* learners in school? Since opportunity, support, and proximity are all stepping stones to the facilitation of friendships between children with and without disabilities, ensuring the success of inclusive services for all children makes good common sense. Jeff Strully, Barb Buswell, Leslie New, Cindy Strully, and Beth Schaffner (1992), all parents of children with disabilities, have developed guidelines that they feel parents and families of children with disabilities might use to help actively ensure a quality education for all. Following are guidelines, similar to theirs, which suggest ways that parents of children with moderate and severe disabilities might act to facilitate their children's friendships in inclusive school settings:

1. Parents can share their dream and the importance of friendships for their child with teachers and staffing teams, school improvement committees, professional accreditation bodies, and school board members by attending meetings and voicing their ideas and vision.

2. Parents can become involved in making social opportunities a reality for their child and other children by getting involved with their own child's education to ensure that such opportunities are available and that classroom practices reflect the importance of supporting children's friendships (see Chapter 10).

3. Parents can provide expertise and talent to the school. They should be involved in the school community and can model through their relationships with parents of typically developing children the importance of interaction between families who do and do not have children with disabilities.

4. Parents can help other parents understand the power of coalitions and the need for everyone to work together for a better school for all children— a school that values each and every child as a contributing, important member (see Chapter 11).

5. Parents should work to ensure that their child's school program is the best that it can be, not only

for the achievement of academic goals, but social ones as well—their efforts will influence others.

6. Parents can support teachers and administrators to learn more about children's friendships, inclusiveness, and quality education by taking people to conferences, purchasing books or videos, sharing information, and talking with people about their hopes and dreams.

7. Parents can advocate for positive change so that their child and the children that their child will meet may have the experience of a quality education in an inclusive school that supports and nurtures children's friendships by forming a committee or group specifically for this purpose.

8. Parents should celebrate the victories, learn from the things that do not work, and commend the people who are making positive changes for all children.

9. Parents should believe in a future not only for their child, but for all children. Change happens when people come together and struggle, when everyone works for a better school and for all children, rather than fighting for a bigger slice of the pie for a specific group or child (pp. 205-206).

FAMILIES OF CHILDREN WITHOUT DISABILITIES: PERCEPTIONS, FEELINGS, AND CONCERNS

As a part of the research that went into this book, I interviewed 17 parents of typically developing children who attended inclusive elementary classes with a child with moderate or severe intellectual disabilities (Staub, 1995). In addition to all of the parents whose typically developing children are highlighted in this book, I also interviewed several other parents whose typically developing child had been identified by teachers as having ongoing friendly interactions with the student with disabilities included in their classroom. The interviews that I conducted with the parents ranged in length from 45 to 90 minutes. All but two of the interviews were conducted with mothers. I interviewed one father and one interview was held with both the mother and father (Henry's parents).

My first purpose for the interview was to gain understanding about the parent's child and their child's experiences with disabilities. Most of the parents I interviewed came from average, middle-class homes and approximately 50 percent noted that their child had attended an inclusive elementary school since kindergarten. The other half were new to the school, or had been at the school for fewer than two years. One set of parents were physical therapists and their child had grown up around people with disabilities. One mother had been a special education teaching assistant for students with severe disabilities for three years. Otherwise, the parents' prior experiences with people with disabilities were very limited.

A second purpose for the interviews was to determine the parent's perceptions of their child's relationship with a peer with disabilities. How would they describe the relationship and what did they think about it? Most of the parents felt that the relationship their child had with her peer was a "helping" relationship. A couple of the parents spoke about the love and sense of responsibility that their child had expressed about her classmate with disabilities. Parents of three of the pairs of peers described the relationship that developed as a friendship in the typical sense of the meaning. They included the mothers of Stacy and Deanne, and Henry's parents.

I also asked parents to share their concerns about inclusion at this school (Jane Austen Elementary) as well as at other schools. The primary concerns expressed were that the classroom did not have enough support to include a child with severe disabilities or that classroom sizes would not be reduced to meet the demands of including students with disabilities. A couple of the parents were worried that if inclusion was not carefully planned for, the typically developing children might be neglected by the teacher. One parent also worried about children being included who might be too distracting and wondered how a child who was very noisy or who had frequent outbursts would successfully attend a general education classroom. Stacy's mother was the only one who expressed her concern, shared earlier, about having a guest who had disabilities visit her home.

Although the interviews I conducted were limited in number and specific to only one school, I believe that the responses the parents shared offer a small step toward increased understanding of how parents of typically developing children view inclusion and their child's relationship with a peer with disabilities. Many of these parents have become powerful supports for the parents and families of the children with disabilities whom their child has befriended and they will likely remain advocates for people with disabilities for a long time. Based upon the findings from these interviews, as well as my many informal conversations with parents of typically developing children, I believe that there are several ways, many similar to the ones listed above, that parents of typically developing children can support the social relationships between children with and without disabilities. They include:

1. Parents of typically developing children can spend time learning about inclusive education and the outcomes associated with inclusive education, not only for children with moderate and severe disabilities, but for typically developing children. They should also ask questions: Why is the child with disabilities here? What are the goals for the child with disabilities? All the children? How is the child with disabilities being supported? How is the inclusion of a child with disabilities in my child's classroom helping or hurting my child?

2. Parents of typically developing children can learn more about children's friendships and the value of children's relationships in educational settings and share their knowledge with teachers and

staffing teams, school board members, and school improvement committees (i.e., PTSA).

3. Parents of typically developing children who spend time in quality inclusive classrooms that are designed to support children's friendships will come to feel more comfortable in the presence of children with disabilities.

4. Parents of typically developing children can reach out to parents of children with disabilities to include them in the school community, to build partnerships that ensure that their child's school program is the best that it can be.

5. Parents of typically developing children can spend time listening to and respecting their children's stories of friendship and interactions with classmates with disabilities. They can take a "posture of understanding" through their child's experiences.

FRIENDSHIPS BETWEEN CHILDREN WITH AND WITHOUT DISABILITIES: OUTCOMES FOR FAMILIES

In Chapter 5, I briefly shared the "spillover effects" that the seven pairs of friendships described in this book, as well as other similar friendships, have had on families and parents. In many cases, parents of typically developing children who have friends with disabilities have followed their children's lead in learning to take a "posture of understanding" in overcoming their fears, inexperience, and misconceptions regarding people with disabilities. This generation of children is educating our generation of parents and families about something that for many has been foreign and unique. In an interview, one father said, ". . . we didn't go to school with full inclusion. . . . If our children grow up with people who are disabled it won't be a problem for them as adults as it is for us." Another mother of a typically developing child shared a story about her first experience in an inclusive classroom. I think her story is particularly illustrative of the impact that her son's experiences had on her own feelings and perceptions:

> The first time I went into an inclusive class was when
> Sean (child with severe disabilities) was there. It scared
> the daylights out of me. I had never been around
> people like Sean before and after two hours my nerves
> were shot. Sean would scream and I just didn't know
> what to say or do when he would come toward me. At
> dinner that night I said to my son, "I'm sorry. I don't
> agree with this. I think those kids should be put in a
> special school because it's too distracting having Sean
> there. How do you put up with him?" I guess I was
> ignorant when I said this, but I just didn't know what
> to think. Well, Jason (my son) got mad and said to me,
> "Sean is a very nice kid and he should be there because
> where else would he go?" Jason defended Sean's right
> to attend school with his peers. I wasn't convinced
> right away, but as the year went on and the more
> Jason talked about it, the more I began to open my eyes
> to this experience. I am so happy that Jason is having
> this experience and I only wish that I had had a similar
> one as a child (Staub, 1995).

Family, Friends, and Culture

Linda describes the day that Molly visited her home as having a significant impact on her and her family. Although she was very nervous that she would do something wrong, or that Molly would be "unmanageable," she came to the realization that Molly was just another kid whose family had many of the same hopes and dreams for Molly that Linda had for her daughters. Linda took it upon herself to learn more about her daughter's friendship with Molly. She began spending time in their classroom observing and helping, and she asked Molly's and Stacy's teachers many questions about inclusion, how they supported Molly, and so on. She also swallowed her initial embarrassment regarding her ignorance of Molly's disability to develop a relationship with Molly's mother, Julie. Julie couldn't have been more elated: "For the first time in Molly's life, a parent who does not have a child with disabilities was interested in my daughter and how she could make Molly feel like a welcome guest in her home." Because of Julie's growing friendship with Linda, who was an active, involved parent at Jane Austen, Julie became involved in the school's PTSA and other committees, something she feels she wouldn't have been able to do without Linda's support:

> Until I had gotten to know Linda, I always felt like an outsider at the school, even with the teacher and principal support that I had received. My four other daughters go to a private school so it was a different thing. But until getting to know Linda here [at Jane Austen], I had always felt like a visitor or guest, never an insider. I was afraid to bring attention to myself or Molly—like I should just be grateful that they are including my daughter at all.

Molly's and Stacy's story is a wonderful example how families can influence children's friendships, and, in this case, how children's friendships can influence their families. Our families and our friends are the mainstays of our lives. When we open our hearts and our heads to appreciating and acknowledging the unique differences that we all bring to this world, as Linda and her family did by including Molly and her family in their lives, we broaden our opportunities to experience new and valuable relationships with the potential to affect our lives in ways not ever dreamed of.

References

Boas, F. (1943). Recent anthropology. *Science, 98,* 411-414.

Buswell, B. & Schaffner, C.B. (1990). Families supporting inclusive schooling. In W. Stainback & S. Stainback (Eds.), *Support networks for inclusive schooling: Interdependent integrated education.* Baltimore, MD: Paul H. Brookes.

Duck, S. (1991). *Understanding relationships.* New York: The Guilford Press.

Harry, B. (1998). Parental visions of "una vida normal/a normal life:" Cultural variations on a theme. In L.H. Meyer, H.S. Park, M. Grenot-Scheyer, I.S. Schwartz, & B. Harry (Eds.), *Making friends: The influences of culture and development.* Baltimore, MD: Paul H. Brookes.

Lynch, E. (1992). From culture shock to cultural learning. In E. Lynch & M. Hanson (Eds.), *Developing cross-cultural competence: A guide for working with young children and their families.* Baltimore, MD: Paul H. Brookes.

Mussen, P. & Eisenberg-Berg, N. (1977). *Root of caring, sharing and helping: The development of prosocial behavior in children.* San Francisco: W.H. Freeman & Co.

Rubin, K.H., Mills, R., & Rose-Karsnor, L. (1988). Maternal beliefs and children's competence. In B. Scheider, G. Attili, J. Nadel, & R.P. Weissberg, (Eds.), *Social competence in developmental perspective.* The Netherlands: Kluwer Academic Publishers.

Rubin, Z. (1980). *Children's friendships.* Somerset, England: Open Books.

Ryndak, D. (1996). Natural support networks: Collaborating with family and friends for meaningful education programs in inclusive settings. In D. Ryndak & S. Alper (Eds.), *Curriculum content for students with moderate and severe disabilities in inclusive settings.* Needham Heights, MA: Allyn & Bacon.

Staub, D. (1995). *Perceived outcomes of inclusive education: What do parents of typically developing children think?* Presented to The Association for Persons with Severe Handicaps (TASH), Atlanta, GA. December.

Staub, E. (1996). How people learn to care. In P.G. Schervish, V.A. Hodgkinson, M. Gates & Associates (Eds.), *Care and community in modern society: Passing on the tradition of service to future generations.* San Francisco: Jossey-Bass Publishers.

Strully, J.L., Buswell, B., New, L., Strully, C., & Schaffner, B. (1992). Quality in our schools: A parental perspective. In S. Stainback & W. Stainback (Eds.), *Curriculum considerations in inclusive classrooms.* Baltimore, MD: Paul H. Brookes.

Strully, J.L., & Strully, C. (1993). That which binds us: Friendships as a safe harbor in a storm. In A.N. Amado (Ed.), *Friendships and community connections between people with and without developmental disabilities.* Baltimore, MD: Paul H. Brookes.

Williams, L. R., & DeGaetano, Y. (1985). *Alerta: A multicultural, bilingual approach to teaching young children.* Menlo Park, CA: Addison-Wesley.

Chapter 10

Friendships in the Classroom:
Supports and Strategies

"Theories and goals of education don't matter a whit if you don't consider your students to be human beings."
(Lou Ann Walker)

The children in Caresville, the multi-age, kindergarten-second grade class at Jane Austen Elementary, spend the last 45 minutes of the school day in choice time. Choice time begins with all of the students seated in a large group on the rug, listening to one of the Caresville teachers describe the "choices" that are available for the day. Some of the choices are standard, permanent options such as visiting the reading loft. But most of the choices are selected to reflect the "theme" that is being addressed in Caresville. This year, the Caresville teachers have based their curricular theme on "celebrating cultures and differences around the world." This month the students are learning about Great Britain and royalty. Consequently, many of the choices available are related to British culture. What better than to have "tea time" at one of the choice areas? Karly, a young girl with disabilities, and Deanne, a typically developing child, quickly raise their hands for this activity and head over to the dress-up area. They "dress" for tea and then sit down to have a proper tea party, complete with sophisticated manners and conversation. They take turns being the queen and addressing each other by "Your Majesty." They groan audibly when the teachers announce clean-up and school dismissal time. At home, both girls will share their tea party experience with their parents and will say to them, "I can't wait to do it again tomorrow!"

Ms. Wood's fifth grade class at Jane Austen Elementary is known as the "Wolf Den." They gave themselves this name after learning the importance and symbolism of the wolf in some Native American cultures. Like the students in Caresville, they too are learning about, and celebrating, different cultures. Unlike Caresville, the "Wolf Den" has limited its study to exploring different Native American cultures, traditions, and beliefs. Each day the Wolf Den begins class with an activity used by one particular tribe they have learned about. They call it the "talking stick." Each morning, the students in the Wolf Den seat themselves in a circle around the rug while Ms. Woods holds a wooden stick that resembles a small totem pole. The stick gets passed around the circle until it ends up with the "chosen" person for the day. In addition to being the focus of attention during the "talking stick" activity, the chosen person will assume leadership responsibilities throughout the day. But it is during the "talking stick" activity that the chosen person receives the most recognition. During this activity, each child in the circle makes one positive comment or compliment to the chosen person. The sky is the limit on what comments the students may make, but they must be sincere, positive, and thoughtful. Although Ray, a child with severe disabilities, is unable to verbalize a compliment to the chosen person each morning, his friend Brittany always makes one for him. When Ray is the chosen person in the Wolf Den, the compliments are sincere and thoughtfully given by every student in the circle.

Down the hall from the Wolf Den, Mr. Hansen's fifth-sixth, multi-grade class often seems to be in a state of controlled chaos. Although each student has a chair to sit on in the room, few ever do. It is much more common to find students on the floor, sitting on their desks, or even conversing outside in the classroom garden. They are also constantly moving. One of the implicit rules in Mr. Hansen's class is to "check it out with your classmates first." Consequently, as students finish their work, which they have often worked on in pairs, they talk to their classmates about the outcomes of their assignment or they "survey" all their classmates to come to a consensus on a specific response. Their school day is filled with interactions with their peers. Nelle and Cole, both students with disabilities in Mr. Hansen's class, are not exempt from this rule. They have come to rely on their classmates for feedback, opinions, and reinforcement for a job well done. It doesn't matter that the content of their curriculum may seem very different from their peers', because Mr. Hansen's students select their own books to read, their own science experiments to conduct, and their own research projects to pursue. The only requirement is that they talk, a lot, about what they are doing and learning with their classmates.

Although the scenes shared above are from three different classroom environments that vary by grade, size, and individual teacher personalities, a common thread runs through them. Namely, they are each supportive of children's friendships. Indeed, Karly's and Deanne's friendship may have never blossomed without opportunities to participate in interactive, playful activities such as "tea time" during choice. Brittany may have missed the occasion to view Ray as a valued, contributing member of the "Wolf Den" without the daily "talking stick" activity. And Aaron and Cole and Theresa and Nelle may not have even talked with each other if it hadn't been for the collaborative goal structures present in Mr. Hansen's class.

Despite all the technology that is available to educators today, teachers cannot "program" their students' friendships. But they *can* build connections to foster and support friendships between and among their students. They can use teaching strategies that encourage student participation. They can arrange for students to work together in groups toward a cooperative purpose. They can model caring, respectful, and interested attitudes toward each of their students. Classrooms and schools that embrace "best practices" toward the support and encouragement of relationships between children with and without disabilities are using the same practices and structures found in any "good" classroom used by any "good" teacher. Jeanne Gibbs, author of "Tribes," a program designed to build community, is encouraged by the recent movement toward quality classrooms: "Programs designed to build character, improve classroom climate, create community and teach the skills of democracy and participatory involvement have become more common particularly as concerns about violence in schools and inter-personal conflict increase" (1987).

Joyce Epstein and Nancy Karweit (1983) wrote a book on the subject of friendships and their impact on children's school experiences and adjustment. At the completion of their book, the authors drew these conclusions: First, the environments in which peer interactions occur (i.e., the classroom) affect the nature and extent of peer contact and the friendship selection processes. Second, the ages and developmental stages of students affect peer relations and patterns of selection and influence (p. 235).

Epstein's and Karweit's findings are exciting for classroom practice. These authors maintain that the evidence and perspectives in their book suggest these important outcomes:

> It is just as possible that peer and friendship groups
> can be positive forces in the classroom and can be used
> to greater advantage in school settings to advance the

goals of the school, the teachers and the students. Instead, by avoiding the use of peer groups for academic purposes, teachers are restricting the educational resources that could help them accomplish particular educational goals (p. 245).

Finally, they conclude that teachers and administrators need to recognize their power to determine patterns of peer interaction and friendship choice. While schools and teachers cannot assign friends, they can influence and alter the grouping patterns and the structures of tasks, rewards, and decision-making opportunities for students to increase their access to, and interactions with, other students. In short, the opportunities established for interaction will be the path that leads to potential friendships and, in turn, to their influences on positive school adjustment.

The next sections explore in detail some of the characteristics of classrooms that are most important in providing and supporting opportunities that can lead to friendships between children with and without disabilities. These characteristics, and others important to nurturing children's friendships in the classroom, are summarized in Table 1 starting on page 206.

Fostering Children's Friendships: The Impact of Classroom Practices

This is an exciting time for teachers in today's classrooms. We are learning much more about the influence of classroom structures and teaching practices on children's relationships with one another. To ensure that all children have opportunities for friendships requires a reflection on our current teaching practices and a discussion regarding the fundamental purpose and structure of today's classrooms and schools. To accomplish this goal we need to:

1. Recognize and value the importance of social context for learning for *all* learners;

2. Structure learning that not only teaches values, but allows children to experience such values in everyday routines;
3. Provide classroom and instructional strategies that foster peer relationships in caring community schools (Grenot-Scheyer, Staub, Schwartz, & Peck, 1997).

While we can create classroom contexts that do enhance relationships and, thus, caring school communities, we can only do so when such schools are inclusive of *all* learners. Following are several classroom practices that are respectful of all learners, that have been shown to have a positive impact on children's friendships, increase individuals' sense of belonging and community, and build students' empathy and prosocial behaviors toward one another. Not surprisingly, many of these strategies were the same I found in the classrooms where students with and without disabilities had entered into true friendships with each other.

CARING CLASSROOMS

What characteristics are present in a "caring" classroom? According to the work and writings of Nell Noddings and Ervin Staub, as well as many others, a caring classroom is one in which students have opportunities to learn about their classmates in ways that honor the full range of experiences and differences that each child brings. The contributions of each class member are valued and respected and positive interactions among diverse learners are facilitated. The diversity of individuals serves as a starting point toward valuing differences among the group. For example, in Ms. Wood's class, the "talking stick" activity honored a different child each day for his unique contributions to the world and his individual characteristics. Ray, a nonverbal student with significantly delayed cognitive abilities who often engaged in bizarre self-stimulatory behaviors, was never short-changed on compliments by his classmates on the day he was the "honored" student for the talking stick activity. Ray's classmates honored him for his gentle touches, his ability to maintain his balance on the beam in gym, and for his taking turns nicely during choice time. Ray's classmates were able to identify Ray's unique strengths and thus celebrate his differences.

Integral to a caring classroom's climate of mutuality and respect is the understanding that all members of the classroom are equal participants. Students and teachers learn that belonging to the classroom community is a right, not something that must be earned. A "democratic approach" to classroom management is used to support a climate of respect. A democratic classroom emphasizes natural consequences that are predictable and logical. In order for students to develop problem-solving and critical thinking skills, they need to know the "why" behind the rules. Likewise, the classroom rules will be much more meaningful when the students actively participate in decision making, including making decisions about what rules to have present in the classroom setting. The motto of Caresville in Karly's and Deanne's class was "we are a sharing, caring community of learners." Time each day was set aside in Caresville for the students, led by their teachers, to discuss and revisit the caring and sharing behaviors the students were working on. Student input was an important part of the process and the Caresville teachers did not establish or change rules unless there was classwide discussion and consensus first.

Ervin Staub (1996) suggests that the childhood origins of caring and helping come from children's feelings of connection and positive orientation to other human beings developed through their experiences. He states, "We cannot teach children caring values without experiences that predispose them to care" (p. 56). Consequently, an important source of caring and helping is learning by doing or learning by participation. Teachers can provide children with significant roles that engage them in meaningful, responsible activities. Having an active role in creating rules and in decision making is certainly one way to accomplish this. For example, in Mr. Hansen's fifth-

sixth, multi-grade class, a small group of students was organized to discuss the importance of everyone's "membership"
in their classroom. At one point, the group became concerned
because one of their classmates, a student with autism, was
being excluded from Literature groups to work individually
with a special education assistant. The group of students felt
this was an important time for their classmate to experience
membership in their class. The group of students expressed
their concern during a daily classwide discussion time. The
students talked about the issues and agreed that everyone
should participate in Literature groups. Adjustments were
made in the disabled student's schedule, as well as accommodations to the curriculum, and he soon became an active, valued member of a Literature group. By allowing his students to
participate in active, meaningful roles, Mr. Hansen established
a climate of respect for all of his students.

Central to the development of a caring classroom is the
promotion of prosocial development. Schools and classrooms
can be structured to facilitate kindness, consideration, empathy, concern, and care for others. One way to achieve this is for
teachers to avoid competition and focus instead on consequences that help all students. For example, students in
Caresville filled in a "caring" log when another student had
shown a kindness to them. When the log was filled with names
of students who had shown kindness, the class enjoyed a special treat such as extended choice time. Students also want to
know how much their teachers care about them, not how much
their teachers know. Authentic caring requires listening, reflecting, trusting, and respecting the learner (Freiberg, 1996).
One way that a teacher can demonstrate that they value, trust,
and respect their students is through dialogue with their students. Evelyn Schneider (1996), who writes about giving students a voice in the classroom, believes a powerful forum for
supporting moral development is the class meeting. She suggests that the first meeting begin with this inquiry: "What
kind of a classroom community do we want to have?" The
meetings, once established, become a regular event. Without

exception, all of the classrooms attended by the seven pairs of children in this book had class-wide meetings on a regular basis. The inclusion of students with disabilities was one of the many issues brought up for discussion during these times.

How does a child's participation in a caring classroom foster his interactions with other students, potentially leading to friendship? In a classroom dedicated to caring, students are encouraged to support each other, opportunities for peer interactions are provided, and the quality of those interactions are important to both teacher and students (Noddings, 1991). A caring classroom becomes the foundation, as well as the guiding principle, by which interactions between students are built. If a child is encouraged to value diversity and celebrate individual characteristics, the opportunities to potentially establish relationships from a wider range of students become possible. Brittany, a typically developing child, was supported in her relationship with Ray by the classroom climate established by their teacher, Ms. Woods. Additionally, specific contextual and instructional features present in caring classrooms can be examined and modified to foster peer interactions and friendships. For example, cooperative goal structures can provide occasions to be caring and respectful of one another.

Working Together—Cooperative Goal Structures

In classrooms supported by cooperative goal structures, student group members are involved in the achievements of their fellow group members. By employing cooperative goal structures, teachers prevent students from being alienated from the work of others by having them work together, or antagonistic to the achievement of others, by avoiding competitive structures (Bryant, 1998). Brenda Bryant has studied children's coping at school, and has found that classrooms using cooperative goal structures help generate friendships and foster the development of a variety of emotions at wide levels of intensity. She states that "utilizing cooperative learning formats is a productive context for facing academic and interpersonal setbacks, using a range of coping strategies, and ultimately experiencing peer and work success" (p. 365). She believes that an important outcome of setting up cooperative goal structures in classrooms is that it fosters interpersonal acceptance of individual differences. This in turn encourages self-disclosure, raises self-esteem and confidence, and promotes a child's sense of personal control over important matters in his life. Furthermore, Dr. Bryant argues that cooperatively organized classrooms can reduce teacher stress by promoting positive, educational peer interaction, including greater acceptance of students with diverse learning abilities. Students support each other and experience a genuine concern about their academic progress, be it success or failure.

Perhaps the most well-known use of cooperative goal structures in classroom settings is the cooperative learning group. Cooperative learning groups are usually composed of a small group of students (usually no fewer than four and no more than seven) that meet together regularly for an extended period of time to accomplish a specific goal. In particular, cooperative learning methods attempt to ensure that each student makes a substantial contribution to the group so that members are equal in the sense of role equality (Slavin & Hansell, 1983). Robert Slavin (1983) has summarized the findings of several studies showing that cooperative learning activities help promote cross-racial friendships, interpersonal attraction, cooperative skills, and social perspective taking. Cooperative learning groups were an important part of Molly's and Stacy's sixth-grade experience in Mr. Page's class. For example, Mr. Page often used "reading theater" as a means for demonstrating the students' knowledge and comprehension at the completion of a novel or book that the group was reading. As the reading groups finished a novel, they wrote a script that represented the novel. All group members were expected to participate in the cooperative activity including Molly, a child with moderate mental retardation who is virtually a nonreader. Mr. Page once wrote about these experiences: "The students with disabilities have shined during these skits. They take pride in their performance and become totally engaged in the learning experience. At times they need prompts or reminders, but their group members take ownership and help each other as needed" (Pernat, 1995).

Participating in a classroom that uses cooperative goal structures allows children opportunities to interact with each other in meaningful ways. All children are considered "equal" and as having something significant to contribute. When children view each other in this light they are much more likely to look past differences and find comfort and pleasure in each other's company. Consequently, the building blocks to the development of friendship are set in place.

Classroom Structures: Environments and Strategies That Foster Friendship

Classrooms and schools may also be organized in ways that either encourage or discourage students from interacting with one another. Even the teaching methods that a teacher uses can draw students together or keep them apart. Employing cooperative goal structures, described above, is certainly one planful way that a teacher can bring students with diverse abilities together. The use of cooperative goal structures, however, is usually a conscious decision on the part of a teacher. There are many other considerations to setting up a classroom that a teacher may consciously or unconsciously use that bring students together in socially meaningful ways. For instance, flexibility of seating arrangements, the amount of space available to carry out activities, placement of the teacher's desk, and the teacher's attitude about whether or not friends should work together are all factors that may influence friendship formation and maintenance in the classroom setting.

Joyce Epstein and Nancy Karweit (1983) have focused on what they consider to be three important aspects of organization that affect students' opportunities to make friends in the classroom. The first is the organization of curricular programs. Are there opportunities available, based on curricular content and design, for students to engage with one another? Does the curriculum excite and motivate the students? Is the curriculum broadly based so that it integrates science, art, music, literature, etc., allowing students with diverse interests and experiences the opportunity to participate? Furthermore, does the curriculum allow for active student participation? Research has shown that in high-participatory schools and classrooms where students are actively involved in learning, more students are selected and fewer are neglected as friends when compared to classrooms and schools considered to be low-participatory (Felmlee & Hallinan, 1979).

The second organizational structure to consider is the organization of the classroom for teaching and learning, and, in particular, the teacher's organization of the task and reward structures. The task and reward structures that teachers use to organize their classrooms determine the kinds of assignments and activities that children interact in, how students are expected to treat each other as workers and sources of knowledge, and how teachers reward students for individual or group efforts. In Caresville, the multi-grade classroom that Karly attended with Deanne, the teachers established the idea that fellow classmates are important sources of information. One very simple way they did this was to set up rules regarding teacher help. For the "ask three before me" rule, students were required to ask at least three other classmates before they went to the teacher for assistance. For the "elbow partner" rule, when students were in need of help, they were to ask first the child next to their right elbow and then the child to their left elbow. In Caresville, the classroom was structured in such a way as to encourage contact between students as evidenced by these examples. Finally, the classroom environment will be more responsive to students if:

1. there are many reasons that students can receive rewards in class;
2. the rewards are distributed fairly;
3. they are based on individual student progress rather than on relative standings; and

4. a variety of types of rewards are given, i.e.,
   special privileges, praise, material goods, etc.

According to Epstein and Karweit, how such task and reward structures are organized directly affects learning and student relationships.

The third organizational structure that Epstein and Karweit refer to is the actual physical condition and arrangement of the classroom space. Are desks and tables set up so students can see each other, talk to each other, and be with each other? Robert Marc (1973) says that teachers should consider every available square foot of legally useable space in and around the classroom for learning activities. There should also be a collection of comfortable old furniture and the teacher's desk should be placed in some out-of-the-way corner. In Mr. Hansen's fifth-sixth, multi-grade classroom, which was located in an old portable building, the students designed, planted, and harvested a garden outside the back door of their classroom. When an old picnic bench was placed in the center of the garden, this became a popular lunch spot on sunny days for classmates to appreciate their mutual hard work. In Mr. Page's sixth-grade class, an old couch was salvaged from the dump and covered with an attractive blanket. Like the picnic bench in the garden of Mr. Hansen's class, the couch in Mr. Page's room provided a relaxing, comfortable place for students to hang out. Many of the conversations that Molly and Stacy shared occurred on that couch. The environmental structures present in these classrooms encouraged student contact, leading to increased opportunities for students to develop friendships.

Teachers as Models: "Do As I Do"

It is not enough for teachers to design and create the classroom environments believed to facilitate friendships among their students, to have good intentions and even the desire for children to become friends. The teachers must also be able to model for the students the kinds of behaviors they expect from them. Teachers are significant adults in children's lives and serve as disciplinarians as well as a source of values. They give instructions about caring and sharing and can encourage such activities through their own examples. Like parents, they can serve as supportive, nurturing models or as cold, uncaring ones (Eisenberg, 1992).

The little research that has been done on the effect of classroom practices on friendships among children suggests that two aspects of a child's classroom experience may be important. The first is the provision of collaborative interactions with peers, as highlighted earlier in this chapter. The second influence concerns the nature of children's relationships with their teachers. Studies suggest that children are more likely to acquire positive attitudes and behaviors when they experience warm and affectionate relationships with their teachers (Solomon, Watson, Delucchi, Schaps, & Battistich, 1988).

Possibly the most important way to promote and support friendships among students is to be a good model. Teachers must communicate to students through their behavior that every student is an important and worthwhile member of the class. However, in order to promote the notion of membership, teachers must share the responsibility of caring behavior with their students. As suggested by Nell Noddings, teachers must actively facilitate the development of their students as persons who live compassionately and care deeply about others: "Teachers have an obligation to support, anticipate, evaluate and encourage worthwhile activities, and students have a right to pursue projects mutually constructed and approved" (Noddings, 1988, p. 221).

Mr. Page, Mr. Hansen, Ms. Woods, the Caresville teachers and many others whom I had the privilege to know, all demonstrated respect, warmth, and compassion for each and every one of their students, with and without disabilities. They designed their classroom environment to promote student interaction and they used classroom practices, such as collaborative goal structures and class meetings, that supported a climate of shared responsibility for the well-being of all their students. They also modeled the very behaviors they expected from their students by working collaboratively with each other and other school personnel, demonstrating respect for differences of opinions among themselves, and acknowledging and celebrating the successes of their colleagues. Just as their students were able to develop warm and caring relationships with each other due in large part to the support of their teacher, these teachers were supported in many ways by their school principal, Mr. Cosby. In the next chapter, the importance of community belonging and leadership at this level will be addressed.

Classroom Communities, Inclusion and Friendships

Certainly many, if not all of the classroom practices described thus far serve as "best practices" for all classrooms, whether or not they include students with moderate or severe disabilities. However, there are additional factors to consider when supporting a classroom that includes students with moderate or severe disabilities.

Christine Salisbury and Mary Palombaro (1998) have studied the relationships of children in inclusive elementary classrooms and suggest that "within these complex classroom contexts, children's peer groups offer opportunities to learn important social norms, to receive emotional support and security, and acquire the interpersonal foundations for later relationships" (p. 81). They identified four factors for consideration in helping educators create classroom climates that support the relationships of children with and without disabilities:

1. time and opportunity;
2. child characteristics;
3. intentional support; and
4. a sense of belonging.

TIME AND OPPORTUNITY

The more time that children with disabilities spend physically in the classroom and participating in activities that their classmates are doing, the more options their peers learn for interacting with classmates with disabilities. If the teacher has created a classroom climate of respect, caring, and shared responsibility, more time spent interacting together will increase student comfort and willingness to initiate contact and help them be more successful in their attempts (Salisbury & Palombaro, 1997).

Children with disabilities and their peers need varied, frequent, and regular opportunities to be with one another. No matter how supportive the classroom may be for building and sustaining friendships, if the child with disabilities is seldom present, he will not make friends in that environment. Furthermore, children with disabilities who do spend the majority of their school day in the general education classroom need to be engaged in activities that encourage frequent peer interaction and general social skill development. In brief, children with disabilities and their classmates need frequent opportunities to be together within the context of naturally occurring activities.

Christine Hurley-Geffner (1995) has studied the issue of friendship for school-age children with disabilities and notes that lack of opportunity is the largest barrier to the development of friendships between children with and without disabilities. She suggests two ways that a child's opportunity to form relationships with his peers is limited. The first is by limiting the contact that children have with one another and the second is by limiting the support the classroom teacher receives to meet the educational and emotional needs of their students, both with and without disabilities. She concludes that "the fundamental principles of access, belongingness, and opportunity seem to be met sufficiently only in the context of full inclusion. In addition, the importance of teachers taking responsibility to help children with disabilities and their peers learn to interact with and relate to one another cannot be overstated" (p. 112).

CHILD CHARACTERISTICS

Salisbury and Palombaro (1997) also found that the behavioral and personality characteristics of the students they observed determined how interested others were in interacting with them. Certainly, children become friends because of a mutual attraction that they feel for one another. The chemistry that brings two people together in friendship often seems elusive and magical. But teachers can help bring friends together. For example, teachers can lead a classroom discussion on the meaning of quality friendships and the characteristics of good friendships. Children can learn and be made aware of the importance of extending friendship to children with disabilities.

Two factors that Hurley-Geffner (1995) believes hinder the development of friendships between children with and without disabilities are: 1) putting an emphasis on changing the child with disabilities; and 2) viewing the child with disabilities as uncapable. She notes that participating in a friendship is a combined effort of the persons involved and that placing an emphasis on changing the child with disabilities to improve his "deficits" will upset the very nature of the relationship. Indeed emphasizing the child's deficits may potentially be the reason that relationships between children with and without disabilities often end up as helping relationships rather than true friendships. It has also been suggested that the skills of friendship can only be fostered among children who are on roughly equal footing with their companions. That is, they are able to regard their peers as equals. There is a belief that some groups of children are simply not capable of participating in meaningful relationships. Yet, as the friendships shared in this book have revealed, children with varying abilities can be close, intimate friends and benefit mutually from their friendships with each other.

Along with providing opportunities for friendship development and acknowledging the unique and wonderful characteristics that each child contributes, teachers can also involve their students in thinking about supportive relationships and friendships as part of the curriculum. This is one form of intentional support, but there are also other ways that teachers can address the unique needs of including a student with disabilities in their classroom while fostering their friendships with typically developing students. Some of these strategies and supports are described below.

INTENTIONAL SUPPORT

Children without disabilities are not born knowing how to interact with children with disabilities. They may need to learn: 1) how to communicate and interact with children with moderate and severe disabilities; 2) how to make accommodations in classroom routines and activities so that classmates with disabilities can participate actively; and 3) how their actions convey both implicit and explicit messages toward children with disabilities as well as others. That is, they may need to be taught that how they behave toward their peer with disabilities will have an impact on how others perceive the child and how the child with disabilities perceives himself. Helping children become socially aware and giving them the processes and skills to act on new knowledge creates a receptive climate within which children can feel successful (Salisbury & Palomboro, 1997).

> *1. Developing Interaction Skills.* One of the most important requirements for initiating and maintaining friendships is to have effective interaction skills. Children without disabilities need to learn the modes of communication used by a classmate who is not using traditional forms of communication. Furthermore, they need to understand their classmate's specific strengths and needs in order to feel more com-

fortable in their interactions. In addition to knowing how to effectively communicate, children at any age need to know what to expect with regards to visual, hearing, and physical capabilities. Children don't need to be bombarded with information. But if they are to act naturally and comfortably within the presence of their classmate who has a disability, they should be prepared for things that may come up that will be new to them. For example, Cole, a student with severe disabilities, also experiences seizures, which are certainly frightening to witness. But his classmates had been informed about the seizures and had discussed what their role should be in the event of a seizure. They also asked numerous questions, which were answered with honest and open responses. As a result, the first time that Cole had a seizure in his friend's presence, Aaron handled it calmly, sufficiently, and respectfully. Having seizures was just a part of who Cole was and Aaron had no trouble accepting that.

2. **Making Accommodations.** Other things to teach students without disabilities may include: how to make accommodations for physical and cognitive disabilities, how to make adaptations unique to sensory loss, and how to understand unexpected and undesired behavior. I have found that when children are given the opportunity, they create very natural and wonderful adaptations for their classmates with disabilities. In Molly's sixth-grade class, her peers, often led by Stacy, found numerous ways to make sure that Molly was included and participating meaningfully in literature groups. Theresa, a typically developing fifth grader, found various ways to communicate with her friend Nelle, who was

nonverbal. Theresa also played an active role in developing Nelle's communication book. These children were able to make these accommodations for their friends with disabilities because they were in environments that supported and respected their ideas and input.

3. *Understanding How Actions Send Messages.* Another way to intentionally support the friendships of children with and without disabilities is to integrate the concept and meaning of friendships into the curriculum. Students are more likely to learn about the complex nature of friendship, respecting others, treating others with dignity, and so forth when the topics are routinely brought up for discussion. Teachers can integrate friendships as an important class topic by developing an anti-bias curriculum. An anti-bias curriculum is one that should be free from bias or stereotyping of any individual or group. It is based upon the value that differences are good and that we should teach children about appreciating differences among people. Teachers using an anti-bias curriculum highlight and emphasize students' similarities, celebrate differences, and provide natural opportunities within the curriculum for students to learn about each other.

There are also several structured activities and strategies that have been developed to specifically address the development of relationships between children with and without disabilities. One strategy is referred to as MAPS, which stands for "Making Action Plans" (Forest & Lusthaus, 1990). The purpose of MAPS is to assemble significant people in a child's life to develop an action plan to be implemented in a general education setting. The action plan can be based on increasing that child's opportunities and means for making friends within the classroom. Critical to the MAPS process is assembling a team that includes family members, school personnel, and two to five peers of the student with disabilities. The MAPS process can be initiated by anyone interested in developing a structured plan for increasing a child's relationships with others. Most often, a special education consulting teacher initiates the process and develops the team, although a family member, a peer, or a general education teacher could also initiate the process.

"Circle of friends" (Perske, 1989) is another strategy that has been used to develop relationships among students with and without disabilities who are included in general education settings. It is a wonderful approach for increasing children's awareness of, and sensitivity toward, the importance of friendships in all of our lives. Once again, this approach is usually initiated by a special education consulting teacher. The primary purpose of a "circle of friends" is to broaden the range of peers that a child with disabilities has in his inner circles of intimate relationships. A "circle of friends" for a child of disabilities is formed and then may meet together on a regular basis to engage in social activities.

Although these two approaches have been widely used in inclusive school settings, there is little research available to support how often true friendships between children with and without disabilities emerge from these types of strategies.

BELONGING

In order for any of the above considerations to have meaning, there must be an implicit and explicit attitude among teachers, staff members, and students that "everyone belongs" (Salisbury & Palomboro, 1997). This attitude is not only a necessary prerequisite to the successful inclusion of students with and without disabilities in educational contexts, but is also the sustaining force that keeps children working and playing together. Having even just one friendship with another child in a classroom can be very important to children's sense of membership and well-being in that setting.

While the focus in this chapter has been on the classroom as a context for friendships between children with and without disabilities, the classroom is only a microcosm of the larger school, neighborhood, and community that a child lives in. The following chapter extends the discussion into the importance of belonging and friendship in the school as a whole and in other community settings.

References

Bryant, B.K. (1998). Children's coping at school: The relevance of failure and cooperative learning for enduring peer and academic success. In L.H. Meyer, H.S. Park, M. Grenot-Scheyer, I.S. Schwartz, & B. Harry (Eds.), *Making friends: The influences of culture and development*. Baltimore, MD: Paul H. Brookes.

Eisenberg, N. (1992). *The caring child*. Cambridge, MA: Harvard University Press.

Epstein, J.L. & Karweit, N. (1983). *Friends in school: Patterns of selection and influence in secondary schools*. New York: Academic Press.

Felmlee, D. & Hallinan, M. (1979). The effect of classroom interaction on children's friendships. *Journal of Classroom Interaction, 14*, 1-8.

Forest, M. & Lusthaus, E. (1990). Everyone belongs with the MAP's action planning system. *Teaching Exceptional Children, 22 (2)*, 32-35.

Freiberg, H.J. (1996). From tourists to citizens in the classroom. *Educational Leadership, (Sept.)*, 32-36.

Gibbs, J. (1987). *Tribes: A process for social development and cooperative learning*. Pleasant Hill, CA: Center for Human Development.

Grenot-Scheyer, M., Staub, D., Schwartz, I.S., & Peck, C.A. (1998). Reciprocity in friendships: Listening to the voices of children and youth with and without disabilities. In L.H. Meyer, H.S. Park, M. Grenot-Scheyer, I.S. Schwartz, & B. Harry (Eds.), *Making friends: The influences of culture and development*. Baltimore, MD: Paul H. Brookes.

Hurley-Geffner, C.L. (1995). Friendships between children with and without developmental disabilities. In R.L. Koegel & L.K. Koegel (Eds.), *Teaching children with autism*. Baltimore, MD: Paul H. Brookes.

Ladd, G. & Kochenderfer, B. (1996). Linkages between friendship and adjustment during early school transitions. In W.M. Bukowski, A.F. Newcomb, & W.W. Hartup (Eds.), *The company they keep: Friendships in childhood and adolescence*. New York, NY: Cambridge University Press.

Marc, R. (1973). *Loneliness in the schools*. Niles, IL: Argus Communications.

Noddings, N. (1988). An ethic of caring and its implications for instructional arrangements. *American Journal of Education, (Feb.)*, 215-230.

Noddings, N. (1991). Caring and continuity in education. *Scandinavian Journal of Educational Research, 35 (1)*, 3-12.

Pernat, D. (1995). Inclusive education and literacy: Engaging a student with disabilities into Language Arts activities in a sixth grade classroom. *Network, 4 (4)*, 12-19.

Perske, R. (1989). *Circle of Friends*. Nashville, TN: Abingdon Press.

Salisbury, C. & Palombaro, M.M. (1998). Friends and acquaintances: Evolving relationships in an inclusive elementary schools. In L.H. Meyer, H.S. Park, M. Grenot-Scheyer, I.S. Schwartz, & B. Harry (Eds.), *Making friends: The influences of culture and development*. Baltimore, MD: Paul H. Brookes.

Schneider, E. (1996). Giving students a voice in the classroom. *Educational Leadership (Sept.)*, 22-26.

Slavin, R. & Hansell, S. (1983). Cooperative learning and intergroup relations: Contact theory in the classroom. In J.L. Epstein & N. Karweit (Eds.), *Friends in school: Patterns of selection and influence in secondary schools*. New York: Academic Press.

Solomon, D., Watson, M.S., Delucchi, K.L., Schaps, E., & Battistich, V. (1988). Enhancing children's prosocial behavior in the classroom. *American Educational Research Journal, 25 (4)*, 527-554.

Staub, E. (1996). How people learn to care. In P.G. Schervish, V.A. Hodgkinson, M. Gates, & Associates (Eds.), *Care and community in modern society: Passing on the tradition of service to future generations*. San Francisco: Jossey-Bass Publishers.

TABLE 1.
Characteristics of Classrooms That Nurture Children's Friendships

Classroom Practices:

- Take a democratic approach to classroom management, allowing students to have a voice in how the classroom is run.
- Give children the opportunity to actively participate in decision making (e.g., decide on classroom rules, determine schedules, etc.).
- Provide consistent, structured times to value and acknowledge the diverse gifts and contributions that each child brings to the classroom (e.g., "talking stick," student of the week, etc.).
- Promote problem solving and critical thinking skills.
- Encourage regular discussions on ability awareness by celebrating abilities and differences that children have.
- Provide children with meaningful responsibilities that contribute to the functioning of the classroom (e.g., feeding the class hamster, passing out worksheets, etc.).
- Expect children to seek each other out for help and support before asking the teacher for help (e.g., through rules such as "three before me" and "elbow partners").
- Encourage children to interact with each other by providing sufficient "down time" and by grouping children in seating arrangements that are face-to-face, comfortable, and relaxed.
- Use structured approaches to fostering relationships between children with and without special needs such as MAPS (Forest & Lusthaus,1990) and Circle of Friends (Perske, 1989). These approaches are used in a way that respects parents' wishes and culture.
- Ensure that classroom aides assigned to individual students do not discourage social interactions between the children and their peers (e.g., by hovering).
- If students need to be pulled out of the classroom for therapy, etc., consider the effect of pull-outs on socialization opportunities.

Curriculum:

- Includes goals that children must work together to achieve (e.g., through cooperative learning groups).
- Is integrated or thematic (e.g., the weekly theme of the ocean is worked into science, math, and art lessons).

- Allows children with diverse learning styles (visual learners, auditory learners, etc.) to succeed.
- Allows for active student participation.
- Is flexible enough that it can be modified if students are having more or less difficulty than expected.
- Includes adaptations that are developed with input from special education staff.
- Includes adaptations that allow students to meet their IEP objectives, but follow the class schedule to the greatest extent possible.

Teachers:

- Recognize and value the importance of social context for learning for *all* learners (i.e., that being social is an important part of every student's life).
- Model collaborative social skills with their colleagues and demonstrate respect for differences among the faculty.
- Demonstrate respect for differences among students and do not permit hurtful teasing.
- Teach children without disabilities ways to communicate and interact with their classmates who have disabilities.
- Are aware of social skills objectives and goals on students' IEPs and work towards helping students meet them just as they work towards helping students meet academic goals.
- Make accommodations in classroom routines and activities so that <u>all</u> children can actively participate.
- Ensure that all students in the classroom feel safe (e.g., by making sure students have effective behavior management plans, if necessary).
- Do not allow any students to be babied or treated as "class mascot" because they may be smaller or have less mature behavior than other students.
- Do not rely heavily on one nondisabled peer to take on the role of helper, tutor, or interpreter for a student with disabilities.

Administration:

- Supports and encourages teachers in fostering the development of friendships in their classrooms.
- Provides time for faculty to visit and revisit the value of inclusion at their school and in their classroom.
- Ensures that teachers have the training, assistance, and guidance needed to teach children with a wide range of abilities (e.g., by

(continued next page)

providing classroom aides or consultation with special education teachers, therapists, and others, as needed).

- Ensures that children with disabilities are included in "natural proportions" in classrooms—that one teacher is not given all the students with disabilities in a particular grade when other classrooms are available.
- Makes efforts to educate the families of all students, with and without disabilities, about the benefits of inclusion for all children.
- Helps reinforce each student's sense of belonging to the school (e.g., through school-wide assemblies, bulletin boards, etc.).

Physical Layout:

- The school building is completely accessible, so students with physical disabilities can go everywhere their classmates can go.
- Classroom furniture is arranged so that all students can move freely and safely around the room.
- Adaptations are made to allow students with disabilities to be as independent as possible and not have to rely on peers or aides to help them.
- The classroom has space for children to "hang out" and interact.

Chapter 11

School, Community, and Belonging

"No man is an island, entire of itself; every man is a piece of the continent." (John Donne)

As the entire community of students files into the Jane Austen Elementary gymnasium this sunny May morning, the air of excitement present seems to be reflected in the brightly colored tulips that surround the school campus. No matter what the weather, however, the Friday morning ritual at Jane Austen always results in this kind of enthusiasm. For every Friday, the Jane Austen community of learners celebrates and honors their membership and participation by means of a school-wide assembly.

The assembly begins with the pledge of allegiance with all 850 students, their teachers, and the principal standing to honor the flag. Then the principal, Mr. Cosby, makes his weekly announcements. On this morning, Mr. Cosby, wearing his trademark "Elvis" tie, reminds the students of the upcoming spring carnival and the annual school grounds clean-up day. This year, Mr. Cosby has managed to get a local hardware store to donate over 50 gallons of paint to update the dingy, outside portables. The children are encouraged to invite their parents and neighbors to participate in the Saturday event. Next Mr. Cosby declares that next Friday will be "backwards" day. Everyone is to dress, walk, talk, and eat backwards. This proclamation brings wide smiles and giggles to many of the children, who watch their principal intently for his next announcement. Mr. Cosby goes on to acknowledge several classes for things well done in the past week. He congratulates Mr. Hansen's class on the completion of their beautiful amphitheater, which is now a part of their outdoor garden, and he shares his pleasure that the students in Karly's and Deanne's Caresville are now "on-line" with residents of a local retirement center.

As he does every Friday, Mr. Cosby ends his list of announcements by calling the names of each student who celebrated a birthday during the past week. As the students' names are called, they stand up to be recognized. Since Karly's birthday was on Tuesday this past week, Mr. Cosby calls her name as well. Immediately after hearing her name, Karly, a child who typically moves like a snail, jumps up, smiling shyly. As the student body sings "Happy Birthday," the honored children smile and blush, looking pleased by the special attention.

For the remainder of the assembly, a designated class will perform a skit, scene, or play that they have been working diligently on for the past several weeks. By the end of the school year, every class will have made a presentation for their schoolmates. Often the presentations center around the yearly theme that the class has embraced. For example, Ms. Wood's class recently presented a reader's theater from a novel they had been reading about a "modern day" Native American boy who lives in a town not far from where Jane Austen is located. Every child, including Ray, who is nonverbal and a nonreader, participated in the presentation. In addition to providing the students with an opportunity to share what they have learned, the presentations that the students collaborate on build each child's sense of belonging and self-worth as active, participating members of their class.

The Importance of Belonging

The Friday morning assemblies at Jane Austen Elementary are one of the many ways that students' feelings of membership in the school community are reinforced. A sense of belonging is highly related to our comfort and ability to take risks in learning, as well as to our ability to forge ahead with new relationships. It has been a premise of this book that having friends plays a major role for both children with and without disabilities in their social, emotional, and intellectual development. Furthermore, children without friends are less likely to succeed in all areas of their lives. Just as we are recognizing the importance of friendships in the lives of children, we are also giving increased recognition to the importance of the development of social networks and feelings of belonging within the community (Billingsley, Gallucci, Peck, Schwartz, & Staub, 1996).

Educational theorists Jean Lave and Etienne Wenger (1991) have written about the importance of people's participation and membership in their "community of practice" and the importance of their social relationships with others, on learning outcomes. When people feel as if they are members of their community and feel an affiliation with others, they will experience greater confidence and will take more risks. This, in turn, will lead to increased learning. The friendships that have been described in this book developed and were fostered in classrooms by teachers who treated each of their students as valuable, contributing members. Furthermore, the teachers realized the importance and positive impact that interactions with each other would have on their students' academic and social growth and readily fostered these interactions by the strategies and supports they provided in their classrooms. Consequently, membership or feelings of belonging, relationships with each other, as well as the development of skills, were important outcomes for *all* of the children.

Just as a sense of belonging may encourage children to seek out others in pursuit of friendship, having a friend or friends may help children feel a greater sense of belonging with others in their classroom and school community. We also know that children are less isolated, more likely to be selected as friends, and have more reciprocal friendships in "high-participatory" schools where the physical setting, instructional program, and school philosophy have been designed to permit and encourage frequent interactions among children in an effort to build community (Epstein, 1983). Research on why children and adolescents join gangs has shown that they are attracted to the inclusiveness of gangs and the opportunity to bond with others (Hasan, 1997). Children and adolescents who do not have an affiliation with a prosocial environment such as school are at greater risk for joining gangs because of their desire to feel a sense of belonging with some community. Just as the classroom environment becomes an important setting for fostering friendships between children, the school environment, led by a supportive principal and a solid philosophy, becomes an important setting for fostering children's sense of belonging and value.

Membership within the School Walls

Schools that model and reflect the values of including all their students as active, contributing members are those that are systematically building connections between the school and the participants in the school community, including teachers, parents, and neighbors of the school. Building such community connections is essential to fostering a sense of belonging to the school community (Falvey, Forest, Pearpoint, &

Rosenberg, 1994). As discussed in the previous chapter, one of the keys to building connections and friendships between children is to ensure that they have close proximity and frequent opportunities to interact with each other. There are also key prerequisites to building a community and a sense of belonging at the school level. These include a strong school philosophy and commitment to building community; a leader who guides, supports, and paves the path toward community building; and opportunities, encouragement, and support for participation in activities with fellow students that go beyond the academic environment.

SCHOOL PHILOSOPHY—A "COMMUNITY" BUILDING MAP

The overall mission in place at Jane Austen Elementary school was to ensure that every student, regardless of ability level, participated as an active, contributing member of their general education classroom. Furthermore, the faculty at Jane Austen were very committed to providing a curriculum in their classrooms that would accommodate all learners, foster friendships, and allow students to participate to the fullest extent possible. Coming to this school-wide pledge was not something that occurred as the result of one faculty meeting. In fact, the commitment grew out of a "problem" that the faculty and principal were faced with one spring several years ago. The problem was that students with moderate and severe disabilities would be entering Jane Austen Elementary in the fall as fulltime members of age-appropriate, general education classrooms. Full inclusion was coming. Led by their principal, the staff and faculty went into action and began planning how they would include these students. The problem soon became a challenge. An inclusion task force, including administrators, general and special education teachers, and parents of students with and without disabilities, was formed in order to create a systems change process to develop a school community that

included and supported all of its students. The philosophy statement that was developed as part of this process reflected the
shared agenda and promise to include all students:

> The mission of Jane Austen Elementary School is to
> provide a safe community of learners that is positive
> and productive, creative and caring, for ALL its stu-
> dents, staff, and families (Gallucci, 1992).

This philosophy, which was developed and supported by
the Jane Austen community, served as the foundation for the
growth of the friendships that are shared in this book. For
without the commitment to include *all* students as valued,
contributing members, students like Karly, Molly, Ray, Nelle,
and Cole may have never had the necessary opportunities to
interact with their peers in the first place. It was these initial
interactions in classroom settings that were supported by the
school's philosophy, that eventually grew and flourished into
the friendships that have been described here. With this perspective, the fostering of friendship is not only important at
the level of child-to-child interactions, but at the top-down level,
beginning with the philosophy and promise set forth by the
school community.

Although it would be a wonderful luxury to write about
the change processes that Jane Austen and other schools have
used to restructure schools to meet the needs of all students,
that is not possible within the scope of this book. However, the
philosophy and shared agenda of including, supporting, and
encouraging all students developed by the Jane Austen community occurred because of the presence of several key attributes that are summarized here:

1. A climate and culture that supports respect and
   collaboration among its members and which
   encourages experimentation and risk taking;
2. Use of knowledge, including research and
   models for effective teaching, and principles of
   adult learning and change to guide in the
   change process;

3. Participation and leadership, involving teachers, parents, and administrators sharing responsibility for the change process.
4. Resources and opportunities ensuring sufficient time, incentives, and rewards for those involved in the change process (Murray, 1993, p. 193).

Finally, it is important to point out the important leadership role that the school's principal, Mr. Cosby, played in implementing the change process and in developing Jane Austen Elementary's philosophy.

SCHOOL PRINCIPAL—GUIDE AND LEADER

The personal and professional philosophy and style of the school principal has a profound effect on the human environment of the school (Marc, 1973). What the principal does or does not do will influence both the quality of the interactions among staff members, teachers, students, and parents and the sense of affiliation that the students, staff, and families have for their school community. In most school systems, including Jane Austen Elementary, the principal or educational administrator is the one who is responsible for publicly articulating the philosophy of the school and the school district, as well as assuring that the actions of the teachers, support personnel, and students are congruent with the philosophy (Villa & Thousand, 1990). Because of his or her leadership role, the principal is in a position to influence the organizational structure of a school and the values of the school community.

During the philosophy building and planning process for inclusion at Jane Austen Elementary, Mr. Cosby encouraged his faculty and staff to articulate and implement a vision of how they would meet the needs of all students, including those with moderate and severe disabilities. Mr. Cosby demonstrated his support by making time for faculty and staff to engage in discussion; encouraging the task force team to work collaboratively towards resolving problems and developing solutions; and supporting his staff members in making important programmatic and instructional decisions related to including all learners. Most importantly, however, Mr. Cosby expressed his support for the inclusion of all students by treating each and every student at Jane Austen Elementary as a valued and respected member of the school community. He made a point of trying to learn every child's name and acknowledge them as they walked by. He spent time hanging out in classrooms, interacting with children. In the process, he also modeled for the children how to communicate with students such as Nelle, who is largely nonverbal, or how to handle Cole's inappropriate behaviors. In addition, he celebrated children's individual and unique contributions to the school community such as Ray's participation in the school-wide recycling program and Molly's successful completion of her sixth-grade community requirement. With his warm, caring, and positive attitude, Mr. Cosby paved the path for his faculty's and students' participation in a warm and positive climate.

In an early study, educational researcher Robert Marc (1973) found that there are some general characteristics of principals who lead in positive school climates such as Jane Austen's. Not surprising, the characteristics he makes note of are not related to good business skills, but rather to people skills—building good, solid relationships with the faculty, students, and families. Marc found that principals in positive climate schools:

- *Model the actions that they wish to develop in their schools.* If principals expect teachers to be involved with their students, they are involved with students too. If they expect staff members to be close to each other, they are friendly and considerate in their relations with staff members.
- *Have credibility as educational leaders by acting as though the main business of the school is learning and building community among its members.* They visit classrooms often. They hold discussions with students. They

ask questions about teaching methods. They
show interest in new educational ideas. Mostly,
they are visible in the school and are accessible
to students, teachers, and parents.

■ *Are face-to-face oriented.* They maintain
continuous personal contact with their staff
members. Not much time goes by before any
teacher, staff member, or parent has the opportunity to meet with the principal. They ask their
staff members how things are going. Teachers
are surveyed and their ideas and suggestions are
acted upon.

■ *Are honest and fair.* Teachers who work in
positive climate schools feel supported and know
where they stand. Principals are willing to
realistically present problems to their faculty
and involve them in appropriate decision-making processes. They are willing and able to
delegate authority effectively.

■ *Are community conscious.* Successful principals develop the ability to bridge the gap between the school staff and the community.
Parents and other volunteers are welcome and
productive workers in the school and they are
acknowledged and appreciated for their time
(pp. 150-151).

In short, a successful principal understands the importance of the "whole" person—the child and staff member who
is satisfied, happy, and fulfilled in not only their professional
or academic lives, but in their relationships with others and
their sense of belonging to the community. The sensitive principal also understands the importance of extracurricular activities and events in the "whole" lives of their students. In
particular, the principal understands how activities enhance
and support the friendships of children outside of school much
the same way as the Friday after-school get-togethers at the

local Mexican restaurant enhance and support the relationships of the principal's staff and faculty members.

FRIENDSHIP AND EXTRACURRICULAR ACTIVITIES

Extracurricular activities within the school provide additional opportunities for children to meet one another, participate in activities of common interest, and learn and practice skills other than strictly academic ones. Extracurricular activities are also uniquely different from activities that children participate in during school hours because participation is voluntary and extracurricular activities generally make a wider range of student aptitudes, skills, and interests visible than is usually possible in the classroom. Usually the older children become, the greater their opportunities will be for participation in extracurricular activities. There are, however, many extracurricular opportunities available for elementary-aged children to participate in, including scouts, sports, swim or skating clubs, church and synagogue activities, park and recreation programs, boys and girls clubs, summer camp, special interest lessons, and after school programs.

Participation in extracurricular activities has the potential to influence children's friendship selection as well. Not only do extracurricular activities provide extra support for children to discover and develop their talents, but they also provide opportunities to facilitate the development and maintenance of children's friendships. Finally, extracurricular activities provide additional information about the interests, skills, and personalities of the children who participate in them. For example, Karly, a young girl with Down syndrome who loves to dance, joined an after school folk dance group that was sponsored by the school's music teacher. The children in the group who were not very familiar with Karly were surprised to see her at their first folk dance meeting. It hadn't occurred to many of them that Karly, a girl with "special needs," might also have an interest in music and dancing. Once the children got over their initial surprise, with the support of their music teacher, they readily included Karly in their extracurricular activity. Not only did joining the folk dance group give Karly the opportunity to participate in something she loved to do, while broadening her base upon which new friendships might be formed, it also enhanced her fellow dancers' understanding of who Karly was as an individual child.

Participation in extracurricular activities can provide opportunities to develop citizenship skills by promoting inclusive participation of children who have diverse strengths, abilities, talents, and needs. Mary Falvey, Jennifer Coots, and Susan Terry-Gage (1992), who have worked with children with disabilities for many years, suggest that educators, parents, and community members use several methods to facilitate extracurricular activities for elementary age children. Their recommendations are, however, not limited to children with disabilities, but hold true for all children. They suggest:

1. Children should attend their neighborhood school so that after-school and neighborhood activities are accessible to them.
2. Children should be encouraged and assisted to participate in activities that are in line with their strengths, preferences, and talents.
3. Children should not be excluded from activities due to skill limitations; instead, adaptations and accommodations should be made to support and enhance each child's participation.
4. After-school programs should not separate children based on arbitrary criteria such as funding. For example, a child should not be prevented from participating in extracurricular school events because they cannot afford to.
5. Parents can become involved in their PTA and other community events that help facilitate their child's involvement.
6. Parents (and teachers) can support and encourage their child's participation in extracurricular activities (p. 235).

Membership Beyond the School Walls

Studies conducted on the social relationships of young adolescents with diverse abilities reveal that friendships between young people with and without disabilities need to be supported beyond the school day to be meaningful, even if educational programs are inclusive (Meyer, Minondo, Fisher, Larson, Dunmore, Black, & D'Aquanni (1998). The researchers also found considerable evidence that best friendships are those that are nurtured outside of school, particularly as students get older. They conclude: "Social relationships do not enter into the inner circle of 'best friendships' unless they represent mutual activities shared outside the school setting" (p. 215).

Although this book has focused on friendships that have developed within the school setting, children's neighborhoods are also important environments where friends are made. Research on children's friendships has recognized that, like schools and classrooms, neighborhoods have organizational characteristics that also affect the selection of friends. For example, as noted in Chapter 3, proximity of families with children is one neighborhood feature that affects children's selection of friends. If children live on the same block as other children about their age, chances are they will play together and some will become good friends. Size of the available population is another organizational feature of neighborhoods that affects interaction and selection of friends. The facilities available in neighborhoods organize potential friends around activities and projects. Neighborhood facilities may include a playground, ball field, skating area, bike path, swimming pool, pool hall, bowling alley, arcade, and organized or informal sports.

Equally critical to building and fostering friendship inside, as well as outside, of the school setting is having a sense of belonging and a feeling that you are part of a community. After all, a community is all the parts of a whole, composed of people of diverse abilities and national backgrounds. To exclude individuals with disabilities from participating in the larger community is to exclude some of the very individuals who make up the sum of the whole. Michael Briand and Jennifer Alstad (1996), who write about care and community in modern society, suggest that:

> Seeing the public as a vast web of relationships in which all of us are inescapably enmeshed, rather than imagining it as a mere aggregate of independent individuals who interact with each other, can help us generate a new sense of possibility that will release previously untapped energy for seeking and constructing solutions (p. 327).

While this book has shared and celebrated several accounts of friendship between children with and without disabilities, the unfortunate reality is that many *adults* with disabilities are socially isolated. It is wonderful that many schools are now taking the initiative to include children with disabilities and to foster their friendships with typically developing children. The challenge remains, however, to continue to push forward and build community connections between people with and without developmental disabilities that go beyond the school walls, so that people with disabilities can experience belonging and membership in all areas of their lives. If this dream is accomplished, my guess is that it is not only individuals with disabilities who will benefit, but individuals without disabilities as well.

References

Billingsley, F.F., Gallucci, C., Peck, C.A., Schwartz, I.S., & Staub, D. (1996). "But those kids can't even do math": An alternative conceptualization of outcomes for inclusive education. *Special Education Leadership Review*, 43-55.

Briand, M.K. & Alstad, J. (1996). Strengthening the democratic process. In P.G. Schervish, V.A. Hodgkinson, M. Gates, & Associates (Eds.), *Care and community in modern society: Passing on the tradition of service to future generations.* San Francisco: Jossey-Bass Publishers.

Epstein, J.L. (1983). Selection of friends in differently organized schools and classrooms. In J. Epstein & N. Karweit (Eds.), *Friends in school: Patterns of selection and influence in secondary schools.* New York: Academic Press.

Falvey, M., Coots, J., & Terry-Gage, S. (1992). Extracurricular activities. In S. Stainback & W. Stainback (Eds.), *Curriculum considerations in inclusive classrooms.* Baltimore, MD: Paul H. Brookes.

Falvey, M., Forest, M., Pearpoint, J., & Rosenberg, R. (1994). Building connections. In J. Thousand, R. Villa, & A. Nevin (Eds.), *Creativity and collaborative learning: A practical guide to empowering students and teachers.* Baltimore, MD: Paul H. Brookes.

Gallucci, C. (1992). *The MESH manual for inclusive schools.* Unpublished manuscript. Olympia, WA: Office of the Superintendent of Public Instruction.

Hasan, H.A. (1998). Understanding the gang culture and how it relates to society and school. In L.H. Meyer, H.S. Park, M. Grenot-Scheyer, I.S. Schwartz, & B. Harry (Eds.), *Making friends: The influences of culture and development.* Baltimore, MD: Paul H. Brookes.

Lave, J. & Wenger, E. (1991). *Situated learning: Legitimate peripheral participation.* New York, NY: Cambridge University Press.

Marc, R. (1973). *Loneliness in the schools.* Niles, IL: Argus Communications.

Meyer, L.H., Minondo, S., Fisher, M., Larson, M., Dunmore, S., Black, J.W., & D'Aquanni, M. (1998). Frames of friendship: Social relationships among young adolescents with diverse abilities. In L.H. Meyer, H.S. Park, M. Grenot-Scheyer, I.S. Schwartz, & B. Harry (Eds.), *Making friends: The influences of culture and development.* Baltimore, MD: Paul H. Brookes.

Murray, L.B. (1993). Putting it all together at the school level: A principal's perspective. In J.I. Goodlad & T.C. Lovitt (Eds.), *Integrating general and special education.* New York: Macmillan Publishing Co.

Villa, R. & Thousand, J. (1990). Administrative supports to promote inclusive schooling. In Stainback, W. & Stainback, S. (Eds.), *Support networks for inclusive schooling: Interdependent integrated education.* Baltimore, MD: Paul H. Brookes.

Chapter 12

Epilogue:
Delicate Threads

"My friends are my estate."
(Emily Dickinson)

As I reflect on my own friendships and observe my children interacting with their friends, it seems hard to believe that it is necessary to devote a book to promoting and supporting friendships between children with and without disabilities. Yet, as many parents and professionals know too well, the friendships we take for granted in our lives are often never realized for children with developmental disabilities. It is therefore with pleasure and celebration that I had the privilege to study and share the friendships of the children presented in this book. Their stories illustrated not only valuable points about childhood friendships in general, but also, I hope, guided understanding toward the unique value and meaning of friendships between children with and without disabilities. As with the delicate threads that are used to painstakingly piece together a patchwork quilt, piecing together these friendships takes time, interest, and patience. The support of the families, teachers, and the principal was paramount in fostering and developing these friendships, but most importantly, the credit goes to the children, who were able to open their hearts and minds to each other. Friends will come and go in the lives of all children and some friendships will have a greater impact than others. But the friendships that were shared in this book will likely linger in the memories, actions, and minds of these children forever.

It seems fitting, therefore, to end this book by sharing some of these children's stories, one last time. The five stories I have selected to share are of the pairs of children whom I was able to follow for the longest period of time and who remained a part of the larger Jane Austen community after my research was completed.

MOLLY AND STACY

Molly and Stacy became friends in the second grade at Jane Austen Elementary. Today, the girls attend different junior high schools as eighth graders. After a rough start, Molly has been successfully included as a member of the junior high school that she now attends. Molly particularly loves her drama and home economic classes, where she has many opportunities to interact with her typically developing classmates. Molly has made some new friends at her junior high school. One of her friends is another girl who experiences moderate mental retardation and motor difficulties. Molly also hangs out with a small group of typically developing peers during class breaks and at lunch. To date, however, Molly has never been invited to anyone's home or to attend an after-school event with these girls. When Molly is feeling lonely, she asks her mom if she can call her friend Stacy.

Stacy, also an eighth grader, is a very popular, well-liked girl at the junior high school that she attends. She does exceedingly well in all academic areas, but has a fondness for writing. Like her many friends, she has developed an interest in boys. But her mother isn't quite ready to let Stacy date yet. Feeling torn between the demands of junior high school and the "glory" days of being a student in Mr. Page's sixth grade class, Stacy often reminisces about her friendship with Molly. When she feels overwhelmed by the high stakes world of junior high, boys, and who is allowed in whose clique, Stacy will ask to invite Molly over. Stacy's mother, Linda, who loves Molly like a daughter, always says yes. When the girls see each other they hug and grin from ear to ear. They make themselves a snack, shoot some hoops, talk abut their different schools, and enjoy each other's company.

KARLY AND DEANNE

This year Karly attends fifth grade at Jane Austen Elementary and Deanne attends fourth grade. The girls are no longer friends, but they are friendly when they see each other at recess or at lunch time. Karly remains a passive, shy child who is easy to get along with. Her interactions with other students are generally initiated by them, but Karly will usually happily join a friend or friends in play when invited. Karly's mother, who is in cancer remission, feels stronger and healthier than she has in a long time. With her new-found energy she has been able to transport Karly to her many extracurricular activities such as Girl Scouts, dance, and basketball. Although Karly's social calendar is filled with her many activities, occasional invitations to classmates' birthday parties, and family functions, she does not at this time have that one special child to call "best friend."

Deanne, who began her school career shy and intimidated, is now confident, social, and outgoing. She is often surrounded by many girls and seems to be one of the more popular in her class. When Deanne was in second grade, almost a year after her friendship had ended with Karly, she entered a school-sponsored competition for unique inventions. Her invention was so unique that it won an originality award and was featured in the local newspaper. Deanne's mother attributes her idea—a special swing for children in wheelchairs—to Deanne's friendship with Karly. She feels that Karly opened Deanne's eyes to the unique abilities and needs that people have.

KARLY AND HENRY

Like Karly, Henry also attends fifth grade at Jane Austen Elementary, although in a different class. Henry continues to struggle with academic work and as he gets older, his learning disability becomes more evident. Henry, fully aware of his academic struggles, continues to suffer from poor self-esteem. Henry's friendship with Karly had pretty much ended by the time the two children went to fourth grade, particularly as they were placed in different classrooms. More aware of their gender differences, the two children seemed almost embarrassed when they would play together at recess during their fourth-grade year, and soon into the school year, their interactions ended. In third grade together, in Karly's presence, Henry was confident and more outgoing. Karly bolstered Henry's self-esteem. Henry has a couple of friends in his current class—boys, who like Henry, seem unsure of themselves and how they fit into the larger scheme of things.

AARON AND COLE

After their sixth-grade year, Aaron and Cole moved on to different junior high schools. The boys, however, kept in contact occasionally, mainly through Aaron's initiative. Aaron would call Cole to see how things were going and a couple of times he visited Cole at his house on a Saturday morning.

During the summer of seventh- and eighth-grade year, Cole experienced a series of severe and dangerous behavior problems. His parents, fearing for his safety, as well as theirs, made a major decision to have Cole attend a group home for two years. The program at the group home is designed to work and support children who have issues like Cole's. Cole, however, was able to continue attending the same junior high, which is noted for its successful inclusionary program. In spite of the behavioral problems, Cole flourished at the junior high school. His humor and his interest in being a member of his school were likable qualities and Cole soon found himself surrounded by typically developing students who have a continuing fondness for him.

Now in tenth grade, Cole and Aaron attend the same high school. Aaron, very excited to be attending school with Cole, has reestablished his connection with Cole by signing up to be a peer helper for him. Cole has moved out of the group home, but is living in foster care in the same community as his parents. Cole is well known in his new neighborhood and continues to be a popular student at his new high school. Aaron likes being a peer tutor for Cole, but even more so, he enjoys the time that he just gets to hang out with Cole at lunch and after school at a baseball or football game.

BRITTANY AND RAY

Brittany and Ray still attend the same class as sixth graders this year at Jane Austen Elementary. Brittany continues to dote on Ray and loves spending time with him. She frets over his occasional seizures and still advocates for his inclusion. Ray also benefits from Brittany's caring ways. He stops to listen when Brittany talks to him, he follows her to the tire swing at recess, and, with a little coaxing, he indicates a choice to her from his communication book. There are very few others with whom Ray will interact. Next year, Ray and Brittany will move on to a junior high school that hasn't previously included students with disabilities into general education classrooms. Knowing Brittany's determination, it is my hunch that this may soon change.

Selected Readings

Friendships and Children and Adults with Disabilities

Amado, A.N. (1993). *Friendships and community connections between people with and without developmental disabilities.* Baltimore, MD: Paul H. Brookes Publishing Co.

This book examines the mutual benefits of friendships between people with developmental disabilities and other community members. Issues such as work and leisure relationships, community programs that nurture friendship, and gender and religious differences are all explored. This is a wonderful resource for anyone who wants to learn more about friendships and community connections for adults with disabilities.

Hurley-Geffner, C.L. (1995). Friendships between children with and without disabilities. In R.L. Koegel & L.K. Koegel (Eds.),

Teaching children with autism. Baltimore, MD: Paul H. Brookes Publishing Co.

> The author of this chapter, from an edited book on teaching children with autism, does a thorough job of summarizing the importance of friendships for both children with and without special needs. She also describes in detail the factors that adversely affect the development of friendships and suggests new directions for researchers and practitioners in their quest to advance their knowledge of friendships between children with and without special needs.

Meyer, L.H., Park, H.S., Grenot-Scheyer, M., Schwartz, I.S., & Harry, B. (1998). *Making Friends: The influences of culture and development.* Baltimore, MD: Paul H. Brookes Publishing Co.

> *Making Friends* takes the reader on a journey through the complex process of how children make, keep, and end friendships—from early childhood to early adulthood. Implications for the community, home, and school are all shared and often through the voices of the individuals with disabilities themselves, their families, and their teachers.

Murray-Seegert, C. (1989). *Nasty girls, thugs, and humans like us: Social relations between severely disabled and nondisabled students in high school.* Baltimore, MD: Paul H. Brookes Publishing Co.

> One of the very first books to carefully evaluate the relationships between children with and without special needs, this book is an account of one school's movement toward integration and what happens to the peer relationships that are developed between students with and without disabilities. Based on the author's one-year immersion as a "volunteer" in an inner-city high school, this book provides timeless insight on these interesting relationships.

Facilitating Friendships and Relationships among Children in Inclusive Settings

Blenk, K. & Fine, D.L. (1995) *Making school inclusion work: A guide to everyday practices.* Cambridge, MA: Brookline, 1995.
> As the title suggests, this is a practical guide to inclusion for parents and educators. The strategies suggested were developed at the Kids are People School, Boston, Massachusetts." Among topics covered are the importance of communication and adapting the environment and curriculum. Particularly insightful are the stories from parents and children about their inclusion experiences.

Downing, J.E. (1996). *Including students with severe and multiple disabilities in typical classrooms.* Baltimore, MD: Paul H. Brookes Publishing Co.
> This jargon-free resource provides teachers in inclusive classrooms with practical information and numerous ideas for modifying the general education curriculum and adapting instructional techniques for learners who have one or more sensory impairments in addition to cognitive and physical disabilities. Information is provided for the preschool, elementary, and secondary school classrooms.

Falvey, M. (1995). *Inclusive and heterogeneous schooling: Assessment, curriculum and instruction.* Baltimore, MD: Paul H. Brookes Publishing Co.
> By emphasizing the development of friendships and the acceptance of diversity within and outside the classroom, this book presents methods for successfully restructuring classrooms to enable *all* learners to grow and flourish.

Forest, M. & Lusthaus, E. (1990). Everyone belongs with the MAP's action planning system. *Teaching Exceptional Children, 22 (2),* 32-35.

> MAPs (Map Action Planning System) is an approach toward planning for and facilitating the successful placement of children with disabilities in regular classrooms. By bringing the key people together in a child's life, an action plan is developed through an 8-step process described in this article.

Gibbs, J. (1987). *Tribes: A process for social development and cooperative learning.* Pleasant Hill, CA: Center for Human Development.

> The author details the concepts and research underlying the Tribes cooperative learning approach with step-by-step instructions on how to build classroom community. This 432 page book includes 165 strategies, energizers, and resources for teachers enthusiastic about building community in the elementary level classroom.

Heyne, L.A., Schleien, S.J., & McAvoy, L.H. (1993) *Making friends: Using recreation activities to promote friendship between children with and without disabilities.* Minneapolis: University of Minnesota, Institute on Community Integration.

> The emphasis of this practical guide is on ways that parents and educators can use formal and informal recreation activities to encourage friendships between elementary school children with and without disabilities. The book covers common obstacles to friendship, strategies for promoting friendships through recreation, and problem solving when friendships do not work out.

O'Brien, J. & Forest, M. *Action for inclusion: How to improve schools by welcoming children with special needs into regular classrooms.* Toronto: Inclusion Press.

> This short, nuts-and-bolts guide to including elementary and middle-school students with disabilities offers

detailed information on developing action plans
(MAPS) for inclusion and on building a circle of friends.

Perske, R. (1989). *Circles of friends: People with disabilities and their friends enrich the lives of one another.* Nashville: Abingdon Press.

"Circle of Friends" is an approach to getting people to think about the importance of having friends in our lives. This approach has been used in many different ways and by many teachers and educational professionals who work with children with disabilities. The main intent is to stimulate thought on the processes of friendship and what it means to have friendships that are organized for a child by an adult.

Putnam, J.W. (1993). *Cooperative learning and strategies for inclusion: Celebrating diversity in the classroom.* Baltimore, MD: Paul H. Brookes Publishing Co.

An excellent resource for the "how to" on building interaction skills among students in inclusive classrooms from preschool through high school. The authors from this edited volume explain how to adapt curriculum and implement strategies to improve the learning, social skills, and self-esteem of children with a range of abilities and cultural backgrounds.

Ryndak, D.L. & Alper, S. (1996). *Curriculum content for students with moderate and severe disabilities in inclusive settings.* Needham Heights, MA: Allyn & Bacon.

The focus of this book is on curriculum and how collaborative teams can identify relevant curriculum content and provide effective instruction in elementary, middle, and secondary general education settings. Chapter 8, "Interacting with nondisabled peers," provides a wealth of information on social skill development and friendships in the inclusive classroom.

Schaffner, C. B. & Buswell, B.E. (1992). *Connecting students: A guide to thoughtful friendship facilitation for educators and families.* Colorado Springs, CO: PEAK Parent Center.

> This short guide focuses on strategies for nurturing relationships between students with and without disabilities with an eye towards enabling them to initiate and sustain friendships on their own. Also included is background information about how and why friendships occur.

Schaffner, C. Beth, and Barbara E. Buswell. *Opening doors: Strategies for including all students in regular education.* 4th ed. Colorado Springs, CO: PEAK Parent Center, Inc., 1993. 54 pp. $10.00.

> Written primarily for educators, this brief handbook focuses on the changes that teachers, with and without training in special education, must make when including students with disabilities. Much useful information is provided about the supports that *everyone* needs for inclusion to succeed.

Stengle, L. J. (1996) *Laying community foundations for your child with a disability: How to establish relationships that will support your child after you're gone.* Bethesda, MD: Woodbine House.

> The author of this practical and compassionate book believes that friendship is the key to happy and successful lives for adults with disabilities. She outlines strategies to help children and adults with disabilities make a variety of deep and lasting relationships with nondisabled members of their communities. Many useful checklists and tables are included to help parents troubleshoot and improve their children's relationships with others.

Thousand, J., Villa, R., & Nevin, A. (1994). *Creativity and collaborative learning: A practical guide to empowering students and teachers.* Baltimore, MD: Paul H. Brookes Publishing Co.
> A wealth of information, including sample lesson plans, illustrative case studies, and hands-on materials are provided in this book for facilitating collaborative learning in the inclusive classroom. By putting a focus on how students work together, a teacher can enhance *all* of the relationships in their classrooms.

Index

About the Author

Debbie Staub, former Project Coordinator for the federally funded research project, Consortium of Collaborative Research on Social Relationships of Individuals with Severe Disabilities at the University of Washington site in Seattle, has spent the past ten years studying the relationships of children with and without disabilities in inclusive environments. She has published several articles and chapters on the subject for both professional and practitioner audiences. She is also a lecturer and part-time teaching assistant in the Special Education Program at the University of Washington and has taught courses in the areas of educating students with autism, inclusion, curriculum design and instruction for students with severe disabilities, and collaboration and consultation among general and special educators. She earned her doctorate in Special Education from the University of California, Berkeley, and San Francisco State University in 1991. Currently a Research Associate for the Washington Research Institute in Seattle, she is an active advocate for children with disabilities. She serves as a special-needs representative for her neighborhood elementary school and she is a member of national disability organizations. She lives in Redmond, Washington, with her husband and their three children.